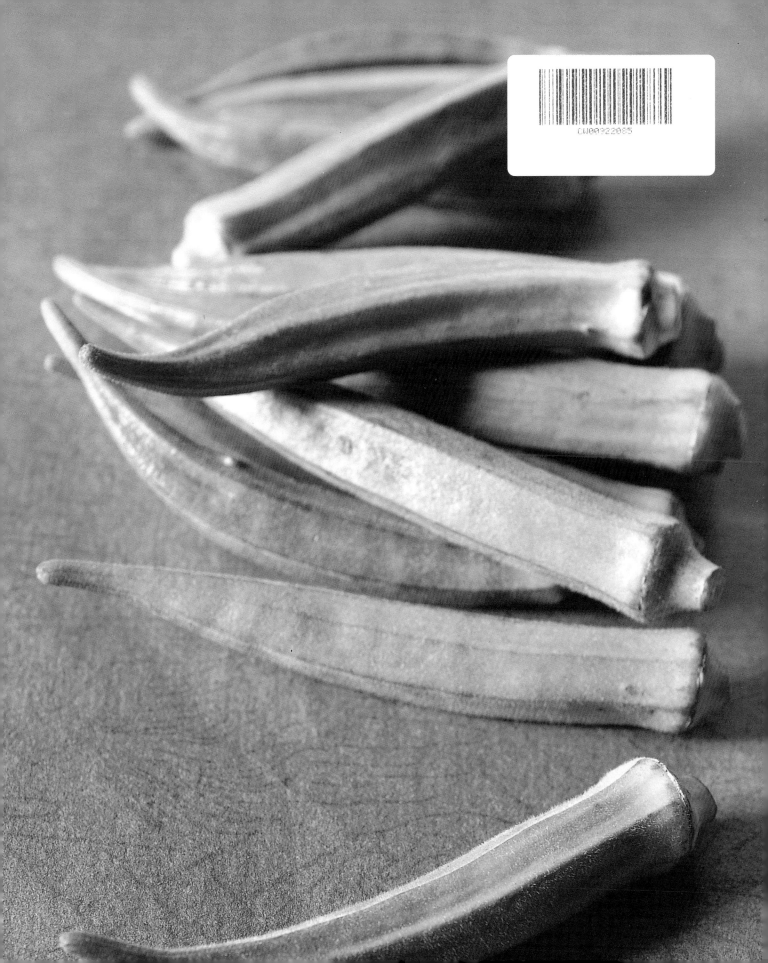

Hiltl.
Virtuoso
Vegetarian

For my family. Rolf Hiltl

Hiltl.
Virtuoso
Vegetarian

WERDVERLAG

© 2006 Werd Verlag AG, Zurich
New revised and updated edition

Recipes: Hiltl family and their cooks
Adapted and prepared by Helmut Schattauer and Sven Zyschka
Styling and editing of new recipes: Karin Messerli, Zurich
Food photography: Marie-Pierre Morel, Paris
Texts and history: Paul Imhof
Photographs: Pages 180, 181, Arsène Saheurs, Zurich;
Pages 182-191, Hiltl family archive, page 184 centre, Thomas Burla, Zurich;
Page 185 top left, Beatrice Niederau, Zurich;
Page 192, Wirz Werbung AG
Design and layout: Scherer Kleiber CD, Zurich
Printed by: Bodan AG Druckerei und Verlag, Kreuzlingen
English translation and editing: Birgit Rommel, Weisslingen
ISBN 978-3-85932-534-0

Contents

* Additional recipes

Food for a Vegetarian Mood

In 1998 the vegetarian Hiltl Restaurant in Zurich celebrated its 100th anniversary; an ideal occasion to publish a book of this kind. At the time it didn't occur to any of us that *Vegetarisch nach Lust und Laune* would be such a resounding success. It was translated into French and English and more than 50,000 copies were sold. Naturally, we were delighted by the tremendous interest the book generated in vegetarian food generally, and in our restaurant in particular. Eight years later we are more than happy to present this new, revised edition of our classic cookery book.

Only ten years ago, vegetarian cuisine still aroused incredulity and scepticism. Bewildered tourists, who had come into the restaurant more or less by accident because they liked the look of it, its bistro style, or the fact that it was obviously popular, were amazed: "What, no meat? And you don't serve fish either?" I understood them only too well, as the word vegetarian hardly conjured up an image of fine food served in a relaxed atmosphere. At that time there was more than some truth in such negative preconceptions.

It was widely believed that vegetarian food was dull, perhaps good for convalescents but certainly not something to eat for pleasure. Today such prejudices no longer exist. Vegetarian food is no longer ridiculous, but part of our culinary heritage; the focus now is on quality and taste, on change and variety.

With or without meat, a good meal depends on the products used and the cooking skills available. My great-grandfather was well aware of that. In 1948, when we celebrated our 50th anniversary, he wrote, "I want everyone who dines here to feel at home and enjoy our wide choice of good, healthy and nutritious food."

We want to foster *joie de vivre*. Our focus is always on people – whether guests or employees. For four generations now, we have combined innovation and tradition. As a team, we try to delight our guests anew each and every day. That's why we're happy to pass on what we've learnt over the years. We've compiled more than 80 recipes, some of which are so popular that the restaurant wouldn't be the same without them. And this includes more than 20 additional recipes which our guests have repeatedly asked for since we published the first edition of this book. We've even laid open the secret of our carrot salad!

This book is also a thank-you to my forebears and all the Hiltl staff. More than ninety people play a major part in ensuring that the oldest vegetarian restaurant in Europe will always be young at heart.

Rolf Hiltl

In the Mood for Meat?

You're both trained cooks, one a hunter and the other a semi-vegetarian – where do Beat Caduff and Rolf Hiltl differ?

Rolf Hiltl: For me, being a semi-vegetarian means that I enjoy eating well and that sometimes I'm in the mood for fish or a succulent piece of meat.

Beat Caduff: I sometimes have a meal without meat, but I can't imagine eating only vegetarian food for the rest of my life.

The approach to meat has changed since the end of the 1990s. More and more people are cutting down on the meat they eat, but they don't see themselves as vegetarians.

Hiltl: That's a reaction to the scandals connected with livestock and poultry farming. On the day Zurich's *Tages-Anzeiger* published a front-page story about BSE, we had a queue in our restaurant that reached well onto the pavement. The main problem is how the animals are raised. When we're walking in the countryside and see how pigs, for example are housed, I can understand why one of my children says: "Daddy, I don't think I want to eat meat any more."

Caduff: Giving up meat is also a result of today's meat flavours. Obviously, after you've eaten a smelly pork chop from industrially farmed pigs or a chicken fed on fishmeal, the natural reaction is to forget about meat altogether.

Could one say that in this respect most Hiltl guests are semi-vegetarians?

Hiltl: Yes. We did a survey in which more than 90 percent of our guests said they ate meat or fish every now and then.

Is that a matter of principle or simply wanting less meat?

Hiltl: Actually, it's both. Some people don't eat meat because they say enough is enough – the way the animals are raised and shipped is shocking: I'll do what little I can by eating less meat. However, I'm convinced that people primarily come to us because our food is good. They come because we cook well, because our service is friendly and because we take our guests seriously. We treat them with respect.

You're saying quality is the deciding factor?

Caduff: And the desire to eat lighter meals. It's true for me, too. I used to use butter all the time; today I tend to use olive oil. And other restaurants, too, have noticed that you can create excellent menus without meat or fish. In the old days they simply served a grilled tomato or overcooked carrots.

The range of vegetarian food is much better today.

Hiltl: It's good, though it could be even better. I once went to the Victoria Market in Melbourne. The variety and the products themselves were superb. Things are in season somewhere in Australia year round. That's a far cry from what we have here in Switzerland.

Do you mean the quality of vegetarian produce here, or the variety?

Hiltl: It's the climate. In Switzerland it's cold in winter.

Caduff: And certain import barriers. Swiss farming is still protected. You can't simply import something that's better. If a Swiss farmer does his job well, he can sell his produce; and if his products are bad, why should the state help him to sell them?

Do you both use organic products?

Hiltl: We use many organic products. Our eggs, for example, are certified free range Swiss eggs; our milk products are also certified organic Swiss. In the case of vegetables the organic products are not automatically better; here we simply go by quality. It's just like wine. Wine simply has to be good. Vegetables must be fresh, crisp and full of flavour. We want to know where they were grown; if they're organic, then all the better.

Caduff: You're one hundred percent right. There are not many aids to help you make a good wine. The only marketing instrument is what's in the bottle, it's the taste. The important thing is that a tomato *is* a tomato and also tastes like one.

People who enjoy meat are attracted by the smell of roasting. It's the so-called Maillard reaction, caused when heat triggers a chemical reaction between an amino acid and a reducing sugar. How can this reaction be recreated in vegetarian cuisine? Or should one just do without?

Hiltl: I know, these aromas wafting from the garden barbeque. I must admit that's a problem. It's difficult to create this effect with vegetables alone. We have a vegetable dish in red wine sauce – a kind of ragout. And the red wine sauce our cooks manage to produce without meat is amazing. I'd say it is pretty close to the Maillard reaction. But otherwise, as far as meat is concerned – and here you'd have to contradict me, Beat – it's the sauce that makes the difference, that and the seasoning.

Caduff: Of course the sauce can play a major role. But remember there are huge differences in the taste of meat, just as with vegetables. I only buy products that taste authentic. They're expensive, whether meat or vegetables. You can get tomatoes for 2 francs the kilo or for as much as 8 francs.

However, you can really taste the difference. For my sauces I use double the amount of vegetables as I do bones.

Hiltl: I'd say roasted onions make a good Maillard substitute.

Caduff: I agree. Essential oils. Shallots; celery would also work. It's not so good with these soy things like tofu. But it's mainly onions that make the difference. Onions give lots of flavour – with their skins, of course.

Hiltl: When we have a barbeque at home we always do half meat and half vegetables. I like the vegetables better all the time; a grilled tomato has a very specific taste, onions too, and courgettes. It just needs a little olive oil; that really brings out the flavour.

In your mind's eye you view the veal chop you've just bought as the centrepiece on the plate, the rest is decoration. How do you create a menu design if there's no meat around which to work?

Hiltl: The focus is on the vegetables. It's a tremendous challenge for our chefs to cook without meat. Of course you also need to know how to make a veal chop, but I'm convinced that it's harder to cook without meat than with meat. It's difficult to make a main dish out of a so-called side dish.

Caduff: You're right. Most chefs find it very hard to produce a vegetarian meal. I need almost twice the time to prepare vegetarian food as I do for a meat dish. Many chefs are not prepared to invest the extra time and effort.

And so they make do with a vegetable platter?

Caduff: Not nowadays. The standard vegetable platter was really cooked to death! They used to put five or six different vegetables on a plate, place it in a steamer and then serve it with a few knobs of butter.

How should it be prepared?

Caduff: Each vegetable needs to be cooked separately.

And the grand pièce?

Hiltl: The first thing that comes to mind is the giant puffball. When my grandfather managed the restaurant they served giant puffball as a cutlet, for example. But you can't find these mushrooms today. And anyway, this would be moving towards meat substitutes, which is not our aim at all. Of course we can offer a four-course meal, though not in the classical Escoffier style with a *grande pièce* – which is out of date, anyway.

Caduff: I'd build my menu along these lines, too, with mushrooms as the main course because they have such an intense flavour. No matter whether puffball, porcini or morels.

Hiltl: Our mushroom stroganoff, for example, is superb!

Today every good restaurant is expected to have vegetarian dishes on its menu. You can no longer take it for granted that a couple dining out both want to eat meat.

Hiltl: Naturally, we've noticed that. There's much more competition today. For me, however, this is a positive development because vegetarian food is nothing out of the ordinary any longer. It has become an established fact, it's quite normal. Today people have a vegetarian meal because they're in the mood for it, not simply because their doctor ordered it.

What vegetarian recipes are there in Swiss regional cooking?

Caduff: There are lots; all those dishes with potatoes – rösti, mashed potatoes – or those with mushrooms or cheese. Cheese fondue is a vegetarian dish. You've got to remember that in Switzerland meat was the prerogative of the upper classes for a very long time. For most people there was only the Sunday roast, and that only every now and then.

So that if we take a historical view, we're not a nation of semi-vegetarians but of occasional meat eaters!

Hiltl: All the same, the range of vegetarian recipes in Swiss cooking – and indeed throughout Europe – is not as varied as in India. It's not by chance that we serve numerous Indian specialities. We look for vegetarian dishes worldwide, particularly lighter recipes. The Swiss dishes without meat tend to be fairly heavy, based on potatoes and cheese. Low-calorie meals are not typical of the mountain regions.

Caduff: It was always colder in this part of the world. In warm climates one automatically eats lighter meals. When I think of Thai markets, with all their fruit and vegetables, then it's easy to do without meat . . .

Hiltl: . . . it's simply a question of enjoyment. It's about good food, interesting drinks and friendly service. About superb quality each and every day. That's our motto.

Soups

Carrot Soup
with fresh root ginger (L)

serves 4

6 medium carrots
1 small onion
2 walnut-sized pieces of
fresh root ginger
40 g butter
1 tablespoon
lemon juice
800 ml water
200 ml cream
sea salt, pepper

Finely slice the carrots, onion and ginger. Heat the butter and sauté the vegetables. Add lemon juice – this gives the soup its attractive colour. Add water and simmer for about 20 minutes.

Blend the soup till smooth. Add the cream and, if necessary, thin the soup with a little milk. Finally, add the seasonings – the soup should taste quite spicy.

Our tip:
You could also add a few julienne sticks of raw carrot. A dash of dry Vermouth just before serving gives the soup a very special flavour.

Lentil and Chestnut Soup

for cool autumn days (L)

serves 4

20 g butter
½ small onion,
 thinly sliced
70 g red lentils
50 g brown lentils
150 g chestnuts
(frozen)
1 teaspoon
brown sugar
½ teaspoon mild
madras curry powder
½ teaspoon turmeric
1.2 l water
1 tablespoon lemon juice
sea salt
freshly milled pepper
100 ml cream
2 tablespoons chopped
parsley

Heat the butter and sauté the onion until transparent.

Add the lentils, chestnuts and seasoning, and sauté briefly. Add water and bring to the boil. Simmer over a low heat for about for about 40 minutes. Add lemon juice, sea salt and pepper to taste.

Blend the soup till smooth. Add the cream and briefly bring to the boil again. Garnish with chopped parsley just before serving.

Our tip:

For fresh chestnuts, make a cut in the round part of the shell. Briefly place in boiling water. Peel while still hot. If the fine brown skin under the shell cannot be slipped of, return to boiling water for a few more minutes.

Cucumber Soup

a wonderfully refreshing summer soup (V)

serves 4

2 cucumbers
2 teaspoons white
mustard seeds
½ onion,
finely chopped
1 tablespoon
lemon juice
250 ml chilled
vegetable stock
sea salt, pepper
fresh dill

Peel one of the cucumbers and chop it into small pieces. Crush the mustard seeds with a knife or rolling pin. Purée the cucumber pieces, onions, lemon juice, vegetable stock and seasonings in a blender. Finely dice the remaining unpeeled cucumber and add to the soup together with small fronds of dill. Chill for several hours before serving.

Our tip:

Add a dash of white wine
or dry vermouth
just before serving.

Vegetable Gazpacho
our popular chilled summer soup (V)

serves 4

10 medium tomatoes
1 green pepper
1 cucumber
1 small onion,
finely chopped
2 cloves garlic,
thinly sliced
3 tablespoons
cider vinegar
1 tablespoon
tomato purée
3 tablespoons olive oil
herb salt, pepper
1 teaspoon sambal oelek
2 tablespoons brown sugar

Make a cross-shaped snick in the top of the tomatoes, cover with boiling water for about one minute and then plunge them into iced water. Slip off the skins and place the tomatoes and any juices into a large bowl or a blender. Finely dice the pepper, peel and dice the cucumber.

Add the onion, garlic, half the diced cucumber, vinegar, tomato purée, olive oil and seasonings to the tomatoes and blend thoroughly.

Finally, add the finely diced pepper and the remaining diced cucumber to the soup. Season to taste, the soup should be fairly spicy.

Our tip:
Serve with croutons. You could also add a little good-quality red wine to the soup.

Salads

Guacamole

as served in "Las Brisas" in Acapulco (V)

serves 4

4 very ripe avocados
1 small lemon, juice
1 small onion,
finely chopped
1 bunch parsley,
finely chopped
a small pinch chilli powder
15 drops Tabasco
sea salt
1 tablespoon extra virgin
olive oil (unfiltered)

Halve the avocados and remove the stones. Spoon out the flesh into a bowl and mash it with a fork. Add all the remaining ingredients and whisk thoroughly.
Serve with corn chips as an entrée.

Avocados discolour very quickly and turn brown and unappetising. If you want to prepare the guacamole in advance, press the avocado stones into the finished mixture and cover with cling film laid directly onto the purée. It will then keep fresh in the fridge for up to 10 hours. By the way, it only works with the avo-cado stones – we don't know why, either.

Our tip:
You could also add chopped fresh coriander leaves and diced tomato.

Chinese Asparagus Salad

an unusual, exotic way
to prepare green asparagus (VG)

serves 4

1 kg green asparagus
2 cloves garlic
1 walnut-sized piece of
fresh root ginger
1 green chilli
2 tablespoons cider
vinegar
1 tablespoon rice wine
2 tablespoons soy sauce
a pinch of brown sugar
1 tablespoon
sesame oil
2 tablespoons soy oil

Peel the lower third of the asparagus spears and cut them into three. Cook in lightly salted water for about 8 minutes. Drain, refresh in iced water and set aside.

Finely chop the garlic, ginger and chilli. For the sauce, mix the remaining ingredients and add the chopped spices.

Pour the sauce over the asparagus, mix carefully and set aside for at least one hour to allow the flavours to develop.

To serve, arrange the asparagus on a plate – or on a bed of salad leaves or finely sliced Chinese cabbage. Sprinkle with sesame seeds if desired.

Carrot Salad

a secret recipe of ours for many years (O)

serves 4

600 g carrots
2 tablespoons lemon juice
1 tablespoon orange juice
120 g mayonnaise
* or almonaise,
see page 154
sea salt
freshly milled white
pepper

Peel the carrots, cut into thin slices lengthwise, and then into thin shreds. Or use a mandolin (slicer) to cut them into julienne sticks.

Stir the lemon and orange juice into the mayonnaise*. Season to taste with sea salt and pepper. Mix the carrots with the sauce and cover for a few minutes to allow the flavours to develop.

Our tip:

Carrots are rich in beta-carotene, one of the four main antioxidants. It binds free radicals and protects human cells. It also strengthens the heart and circulation.

Taboulé
Hiltl style (VG)

serves 4

400 g couscous
2 teaspoons ground cumin
1 teaspoon sambal oelek
2 teaspoons mild paprika
sea salt
freshly milled pepper
400 ml water
100 ml olive oil
4-5 tablespoons lemon juice
½ onion, finely chopped
a little fresh mint, finely chopped

Mix the couscous with the spices. Bring 400 ml to the boil and then cool down to 40°C. Stir the olive oil and lemon juice into the water and pour over the couscous. Mix thoroughly and leave at room temperature for 10 minutes. Sir in the onion and mint.

Our tip:

As a starter, this will be enough for 6 – 8 servings. Originally, taboulé was made with bulgur, which is coarser and made of hard wheat. The grain was boiled briefly, drained, and dried in the sun. It was then milled, sometimes even stone-ground. Bulgur has a nutty cereal flavour and is available in differing levels of milling – from fine to coarse. It is stocked in health food stores, or in Turkish and Greek grocery stores.

Fennel and Apple Salad

a powerful combination (L)

serves 4

1 lemon, juice
2 medium apples
2 medium fennel bulbs
1 tablespoon sunflower oil
2 teaspoons mild madras
curry powder
1 teaspoon turmeric
180 g yoghurt
sea salt
brown sugar

Pour the lemon juice into a bowl. Without peeling them, coarsely grate the washed apples directly into the bowl. Cut the fennel into small julienne sticks and add them to the apples.

Sauté the turmeric and curry powder in the oil very briefly. The timing is important because curry becomes bitter if overheated or cooked for too long. Immediately add this mixture and the yoghurt to the apples and fennel. Season to taste with sugar and sea salt.

Our tip:

Don't discard the fennel leaves, they're edible and look good as a garnish for the salad.

Orange Salad with Dates

refreshing, and rich in vitamins (V)

serves 4

4 oranges
20 dates
200 ml orange juice
a dash of orange blossom
water
a pinch of ground
cinnamon
a few fresh mint leaves

Peel the oranges with a sharp knife, taking care to remove all the pith. Cut into 5 mm slices. Halve and stone the dates. If necessary cut into strips.

Arrange the slices on a plate and scatter the dates over them. Mix the orange juice, orange blossom water and the ground cinnamon. Pour over the oranges and garnish with mint.

Our tip:

Dried dates are very sweet and sticky. In the winter one can buy fresh (deep frozen) dates, which are not so sweet and have much more bite. They're superb with the sweet, fruity flavour of the oranges.

Thai Salad

Leek Salad

Leek Salad

here's how we make raw leeks less aggressive (LO)

serves 4

2 tablespoons sultanas
50 ml apple juice
300 g leeks
180 g yoghurt
2 tablespoons mayonnaise
* or almonaise,
see page 154
sea salt
freshly milled pepper
5 drops Tabasco

Soak the sultanas in the apple juice for about an hour. Cut the leek into fine strips. Wash in a colander or sieve and drain well. Mix all the ingredients and season to taste; this salad should be spicy. Leave on one side for 10 minutes before serving to allow the flavours to develop.

Our tip:

Use bleached leeks. These are available throughout winter and taste milder.

Thai Salad

refreshingly exotic and colourful (VG)

serves 4

1 medium cucumber
1 yellow pepper
1 red pepper
2 spring onions
300 g oyster mushrooms
2 tablespoons
groundnut oil
2 tablespoons
sesame oil
1 clove garlic
sea salt

Sauce:
2 tablespoons lemon juice
2 tablespoons soy sauce
sea salt, brown sugar
5 peppermint leaves

Peel the cucumbers if desired and cut into 5 mm slices. Cut the peppers into strips and the spring onions into fine rings. Clean the mushrooms – only wash them if it is really necessary – and then break them into pieces. Heat the groundnut and sesame oils and fry the mushrooms. Add the crushed garlic and season with sea salt. Spoon the mushrooms out of the pan and reserve. Mix all the sauce ingredients together. Cut the mint leaves into fine strips and add to the sauce. Mix in the cucumber, pepper, spring onions and the fried mushrooms. Set aside for about 10 minutes before serving to allow the flavours to develop.

Our tip:
You could fry the mushrooms a day earlier and store them in the fridge overnight.

Pumpkin Salad

brightens up the range of winter salads (V)

serves 4

3 tablespoons sultanas
3 (eating) apples
600 g pumpkin (peeled and seeded)
200 ml orange juice
50 ml lemon juice
sea salt

Soak the sultanas in water or orange liqueur for a few hours before preparing the salad.
Wash and core the apples and grate them and the pumpkin coarsely. Immediately mix with the orange and lemon juice. Season with sea salt to taste.

Our tip:

Pumpkin seeds are a delicacy if you wash them thoroughly, then shell and briefly toast them in a non-stick pan without adding any fat.
Then use them as a garnish for the salad. Of course, you can also use bought pumpkin seeds.

Sweet Potato Salad

something to pamper your palate (V)

serves 4

6 medium sweet potatoes
2 tablespoons soy oil
1 medium onion, finely
chopped
a small pinch of saffron
1 teaspoon mild paprika
2 teaspoons ground
coriander
1 teaspoon ground cumin
a little fresh root ginger
root
sea salt
½ lemon, juice and rind
200 ml water

Boil the sweet potatoes until they are just tender – about 25 minutes, depending on size. Pour off the water and peel as soon as they have cooled down enough to handle. Cut into bite-sized pieces.

Sweat the onions in soy oil, add the spices, and mix well. Add the lemon juice and water, bring to the boil, reduce briefly and pour over the potatoes. Mix very carefully.

Set aside for 30 minutes to allow the flavours to develop and serve lukewarm.

Our tip:
The red-fleshed sweet potatoes taste best. This salad could also be prepared a day in advance and stored in the fridge. Leave at room temperature an hour before serving.

Chickpea Salad

a taste of India (LO)

serves 4

320 g chickpeas
1 small onion, stuck with
2 cloves and 2 bay leaves
1 teaspoon salt
1 tablespoon
groundnut oil
2 teaspoons cumin seeds
1 teaspoon ground
coriander
1 teaspoon mild madras
curry powder
2 teaspoons turmeric
sea salt
50 ml water
1 medium carrot
1 small onion, finely
chopped
180 g yoghurt
1 tablespoon lemon juice
1 tablespoon mayonnaise
* or almonaise,
see page 154
1 tablespoon mustard

The previous day: Pick over the chickpeas (there are sometimes small stones in them), wash thoroughly, and leave to soak overnight in three times their volume of cold water.

The next day: Add the onion and salt to the chickpeas in their water and simmer until tender. This should take about 90 minutes. Drain in a colander. Heat the groundnut oil and gently fry the cumin seeds until they smell aromatic. Be careful not to let them burn. Take the pan off the heat and mix in the rest of the spices. Immediately add the water so that the spices do not become bitter. Stir this spice mixture into the well-drained chickpeas and set aside to cool down.

Peel and grate the carrot. Add to the chickpeas together with the onion, yoghurt, lemon juice, mayonnaise* and mustard. Mix thoroughly and let the flavours develop for about 30 minutes before serving.

Our tip:
Chickpeas are very nutritious and, if you like them, this dish can stand alone as a main meal. But it can also be served as an entrée for a dinner-party, because it really is something special.

Nepali Lentil Salad
well worth the extra effort (L)

serves 4

150 g brown lentils
150 g urid dal (small
white lentils)
1 l water

2 red peppers
1 small green chilli
1 medium aubergine
½ leek
3 tablespoons
groundnut oil
2 teaspoons cumin seeds
1 clove garlic, crushed
1 walnut-sized piece of
fresh root ginger, finely
chopped
sea salt
1 teaspoon ground
coriander
freshly milled pepper
1 tablespoon lemon juice
1 teaspoon brown sugar
400 ml water
100 ml milk

Boil the lentils for approximately 20 minutes until soft. Pour off the water, rinse with cold water and drain well.

Cut the red peppers into thin strips. Finely chop the chilli. Dice the aubergine and cut the leek into strips.

Heat the oil and briefly sweat the cumin seeds. Add the peppers, chilli, aubergine, leek, garlic and ginger. Season with sea salt, coriander and pepper. Add the lemon juice, sugar and water, and simmer gently for about 10 minutes until the vegetables are tender. Mix in the cooked lentils and add the milk. Do not bring back to the boil. Serve lukewarm.

Our tip:
You can vary the consistency of this dish: add more water, and you have a soup; less water, and the dish has the texture of a stew. Lentil dishes, called dals in India, are eaten there daily and served with basmati rice. They are particularly important for a nutritious vegetarian diet because, among other things, they have a high protein content, similar to that of meat.

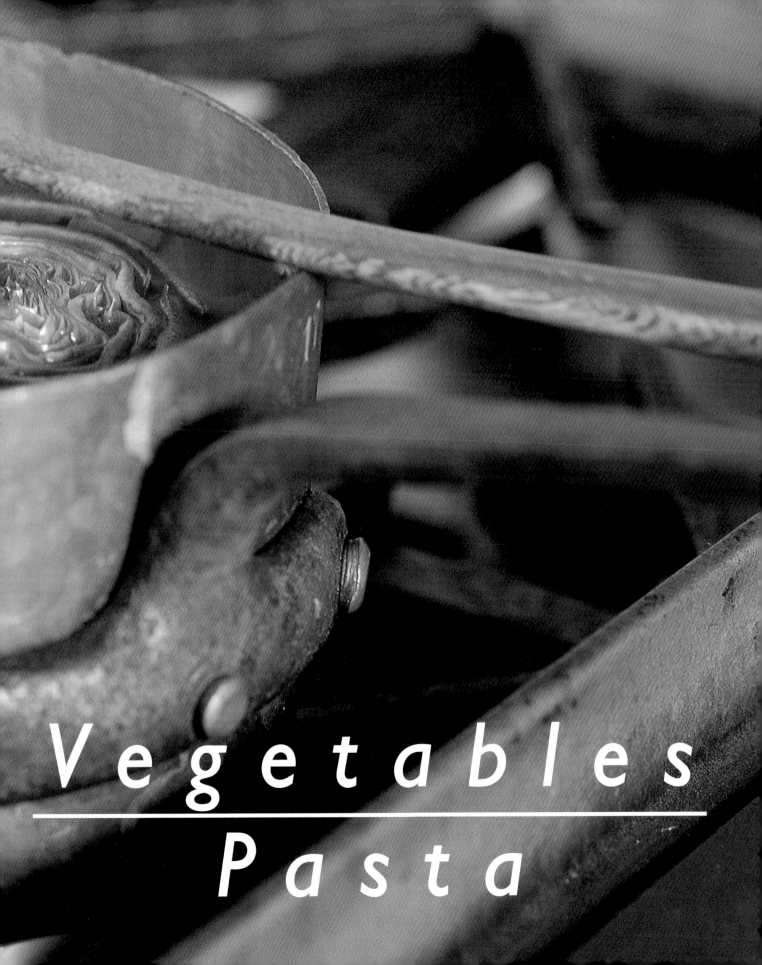

Vegetables
Pasta

Saffron Artichokes
delicious (V)

serves 4

4 small carrots
800 g artichoke bases
(also tinned)
50 ml olive oil
1 small onion, finely
chopped
1 clove garlic, crushed
sea salt, freshly milled
pepper
a small pinch of ground
saffron
1 tablespoon cider vinegar
200 ml water
1 teaspoon corn flour
a few saffron threads

Finely slice the carrots. Halve the artichoke bases. Heat the olive oil and sauté the onion, garlic and carrot. First add the artichoke bases, then the spices, vinegar and water and bring to the boil. Thicken slightly with corn flour. Sprinkle with saffron threads before serving.

Our tip:

We serve this dish in a rice ring with a spoon of sour cream. Restaurant suppliers provide frozen artichoke bases but, when making this dish at home, we recommend that you either cook fresh artichokes and then remove the bases, or buy them tinned.

Ratatouille

with lots of fresh herbs from the garden (V)

serves 4

400 g tomatoes
1 aubergine
sea salt
2–3 courgettes (350 g)
1 pepper
6 tablespoons olive oil
1 medium onion, cut in strips
1 clove garlic, crushed
2 tablespoons tomato purée
400 ml water
freshly milled pepper
1 sprig each of rosemary, oregano, thyme, basil and marjoram, finely chopped

Briefly plunge the tomatoes into boiling water, drain and refresh in cold water. Slip off their skins, halve them, remove seeds and chop into small pieces. Cut the aubergine into 1.5 cm dice. Mix with sea salt, place into a sieve or colander and leave for 20 minutes. Pat dry with kitchen paper. Cut the courgette and peppers into 1.5 cm pieces.

Heat 3 tablespoons of olive oil and stir-fry the vegetables. Remove and set aside.

Heat the remaining olive oil. Sauté the onion and garlic until transparent. Add the tomato purée and sauté a little longer. Add the tomatoes and water, and season to taste with sea salt and pepper. Simmer over a low heat for about 40 minutes.

Add the vegetables and herbs, and bring to the boil briefly. This ratatouille is excellent with gorgonzola polenta (see page 85).

Our tip:

It's a good idea to make twice the quantity: Ratatouille makes a superb cold starter with crostini, or it can be puréed and served hot or cold as a soup.

Cucumber and Tomato Ragout

for people who want to try something really special (L)

serves 4

2 medium cucumbers
2 red peppers
6 tomatoes
40 g butter
2 small onions, finely
chopped
2 cloves garlic, crushed
sea salt, white pepper
1 teaspoon mild paprika
2 teaspoons brown sugar
200 ml white wine
2 tubs sour cream
1 bunch dill

Peel and dice the cucumbers, seed and dice the peppers, dice the tomatoes without seeding them. Heat the butter and sauté the onions and garlic. Add the cucumber and pepper dice and sauté a little longer. Season, then add the white wine and simmer briefly – the cucumbers should still be slightly crisp.
Add the tomatoes and bring to the boil to reduce the liquid. Finally, add the sour cream and remove from the heat – otherwise the sauce will curdle. Sprinkle sprigs of fresh dill over the vegetables.

Our tip:
This dish is absolutely superb with fish poached in white wine, but is also delicious served on a bed of rice.

Vegetable Stew
a dish for all seasons (L)

serves 4

1 medium onion
3 small carrots
1 head celery
1 medium kohlrabi
½ small savoy cabbage
2 peppers (red, yellow)
2 medium courgettes
40 g butter
2 garlic cloves, crushed
200 ml water
100 ml white wine
sea salt
white pepper
150 g snow peas
1 bunch parsley, finely chopped
1 bunch chives, finely snipped

Peel the onions and cut them into quarters, then halve the quarters. Cut the carrots diagonally into 1 cm slices and the celery into 2 cm lengths. Cut the kohlrabi into julienne sticks and the cabbage and peppers into 2 cm slices. Slice the courgettes.

Heat the butter and sauté the garlic and onions, then add the carrots and celery. After approximately 5 minutes add the kohlrabi, cabbage and peppers. Finally, add the water, wine and seasoning and let the stew simmer gently.

As soon as the vegetables are just tender, add the courgettes and the snow peas. Cover, and allow to simmer briefly. Sprinkle with parsley and chives before serving.

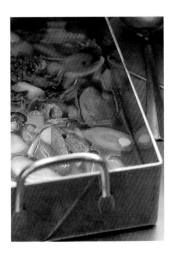

Our tip:

Create your own favourite combination of vegetables, depending on what's in season! Remember that the cooking time for different vegetables varies – the lower the water content of the vegetable, the longer it will take to cook.

Here's what the professionals do: They simply chop vegetables that take longer to cook into smaller pieces than those that need less time. Potatoes fried with fresh rosemary make a good side dish for this stew.

Provencal Potatoes

a Mediterranean stew (L)

serves 4

500 g waxy potatoes
sea salt
400 g tomatoes
1 large yellow pepper
2 tablespoons olive oil
2 garlic cloves, finely sliced
2 tablespoons tomato purée
1 small sprig each of thyme, marjoram and rosemary, just the leaves
1 teaspoon mild paprika
1 teaspoon brown sugar
freshly milled pepper
100 ml red wine
500 ml water
2 tablespoons olive oil
2 tablespoons crème fraîche
a little flat-leaf parsley, finely chopped

Peel the potatoes and cut them into 6 mm slices. Boil in lightly salted water till just tender. Pour off water and drain thoroughly. Set aside.

Plunge the tomatoes into boiling water, then rinse them under cold water. Slip off the skins, remove seeds and chop into small pieces. Halve the peppers, remove the seeds and cut into 2 cm squares. Heat the olive oil and gently brown the garlic. Add the tomato purée and sauté. Then add the tomatoes, herbs and seasoning and sauté briefly. Pour in the red wine and reduce. Add the water and simmer over a low heat for 15 minutes. Then purée the sauce.

Heat the olive oil and stir-fry the potatoes. Add the peppers, fry briefly and mix into the sauce.

Just before serving, stir in the crème fraîche and sprinkle with the chopped parsley.

Asparagus with Mascarpone Sauce

a light dish with a touch of spring about it (L)

serves 4

1 kg green asparagus
lemon juice
sea salt
1 tablespoon brown sugar
1 tomato
50 g butter
1 small onion, finely
chopped
100 ml dry white wine
200 ml water
1 tablespoon lemon juice
¼ teaspoon ground
nutmeg
sea salt
freshly milled pepper
200 ml milk
150 ml cream
150 g mascarpone

Trim the asparagus and, if necessary, peel the lower third of the spears. Bring the water to the boil and add lemon juice, sea salt and sugar. Cook the asparagus until just tender. Remove the asparagus, refresh and drain thoroughly. Then cut the asparagus spears into 5 cm lengths and set aside.

Plunge the tomatoes into boiling water, and then rinse them under cold water. Slip off the skins, halve them, remove seeds and chop into small pieces. Heat the butter and sweat the onions until transparent. Pour in the white wine and allow it to reduce. Add the water and flavour with lemon juice, nutmeg, sea salt and pepper to taste. Then purée the sauce.

Add the milk, cream and mascarpone. Boil until the sauce thickens stirring all the time. Mix in the asparagus and the tomatoes and heat up briefly. Serve with rice.

Our tip:

This asparagus fricassee can also be served as a gratin. Prepare as described and then pour it into a greased, ovenproof dish. Sprinkle with grated gruyere and brown briefly under the preheated grill.

Pepper and Apple Goulash

an unusual and unbeatable combination (L)

serves 4

1 small onion
3 peppers (red, green, yellow)
3 apples
20 g butter
1 clove garlic, crushed
1 teaspoon brown sugar
2 teaspoons mild paprika
a small pinch of chilli powder
sea salt
freshly milled pepper
50 ml cider vinegar
100 ml white wine
approx. 200 ml cream
1 bunch chives, finely snipped

Peel the onions and cut them into quarters, then halve the quarters. Cut the peppers into fine strips. Peel the apples, cut into wedges and core. Slightly sour apples, though seasonal, are best for this recipe. Golden Delicious are available all year round, but are somewhat sweet.

Heat the butter and sauté the onions and garlic, then add the peppers. After about 5 minutes add the sugar, paprika and apples. Season with chilli, salt, pepper, vinegar and white wine. Bring to the boil and reduce the liquids. Add cream till the desired consistency is reached. Serve sprinkled with chives.

Pasta or mashed potatoes make a good side dish.

Caponata
Sicilian ratatouille (V)

serves 4

2 medium onions
2 peppers (red and yellow)
2 small courgettes
1 aubergine
1 small head celery
2 tomatoes
50 ml olive oil
2 cloves garlic, crushed
1 tablespoon tomato purée
1 tablespoon cider vinegar
100 ml red wine
300 ml water
2 tablespoons brown sugar
sea salt, freshly milled pepper
5 drops Tabasco
18 black olives, pitted
4 tablespoons capers
fresh oregano

Peel the onions and cut them into quarters, then halve the quarters. Cut the peppers into strips, the courgettes into 1.5 cm slices and the aubergine into small dice. Cut the celery into 1 cm lengths and the tomatoes into eight wedges.

Heat the olive oil. Sweat the onions and garlic, add the celery and sauté for about 3 minutes. Mix in the tomato purée and sauté briefly, then add the remaining vegetables. Pour in the vinegar and red wine, bring to the boil, reduce the liquids a little and then add the water. Add sugar and seasonings, and cook for about 5 minutes, stirring occasionally.

Lastly, add the olives and capers. Sprinkle with freshly chopped oregano just before serving.

Our tip:
Serve with wholemeal penne or basil noodles.

White Peppers
something really special (V)

serves 4

500 g cecei (long, slender, pale green peppers)
1 small red pepper
1 medium aubergine
½ teaspoon sea salt
450 g tomatoes
3 tablespoons olive oil
2-3 onions, finely chopped
3 cloves garlic, thinly sliced
2 tablespoons tomato purée
2 tablespoons balsamic vinegar
1 tablespoon brown sugar
sea salt
freshly milled pepper
600 ml water
3 tablespoons olive oil
50 g black olives, pitted
1 sprig each of rosemary, basil, oregano and thyme, finely chopped

Cut each cecei into three wide rings. Halve and seed the red pepper, and cut into small dice. Cut the aubergine into 1.5 cm dice, mix them with the sea salt, place in a sieve and leave to draw for 20 minutes. Then pat dry with kitchen paper. Plunge the tomatoes into boiling water, and then rinse them under cold water. Slip off the skins, halve them, remove seeds and chop into small pieces.

Heat the olive oil. Gently fry the onions, garlic and diced red pepper. Add the tomatoes, tomato purée, balsamic vinegar, brown sugar, sea salt and freshly milled pepper. Pour in the water and leave to simmer on a low heat for 15 minutes. Then purée the sauce. Heat the olive oil and gently stir-fry the cecei rings and diced aubergine. Add to the sauce together with the olives and simmer for 5 minutes. Sprinkle with the chopped herbs. Spinach noodles make a good side dish.

Courgettes with Saffron Sauce

a sophisticated dish with subtle flavours (L)

serves 4

650 g courgettes
1–2 carrots
2 tablespoons olive oil
1 medium onion, sliced
1 clove garlic, finely
chopped
2 pinches saffron
a little brown sugar
sea salt
freshly milled pepper
200 ml dry white wine
300 ml milk
300 ml cream

Cut the courgettes into 2 cm cubes. Peel the carrots and cut into julienne sticks.

Heat the olive oil and sweat the onion and garlic. Add saffron, sugar, sea salt and pepper. Pour in white wine and allow it to reduce.

Add the milk and the cream. Simmer over a low heat until the sauce is smooth. Mix in the courgettes and the carrots and cook till just tender. Serve with rice prepared with saffron threads.

Our tip:

If the sauce is too thin, either simmer a little longer or bind it with a little cornflour stirred into some liquid.

Aubergine Fricassée
tastes best with tomatoes ripened in the sun (L)

serves 4

500 g aubergines
1 teaspoon sea salt
100 ml olive oil
400 g ripe tomatoes
20 g butter
1 medium onion, finely
chopped
1 small sprig each of
marjoram, thyme,
oregano, finely chopped
3 tablespoons tomato
purée
100 ml dry white wine
100 ml cream
150 ml water
sea salt
½ teaspoon brown sugar
freshly milled pepper

Cut the aubergines into 1.5 cm cubes and mix with the sea salt. Place in a sieve or colander and leave to draw for 20 minutes. Pat dry with kitchen paper. Heat the olive oil and gently stir-fry the aubergines. Remove from pan and set aside.

Plunge the tomatoes into boiling water, and then rinse them under cold water. Slip off the skins, halve them, remove seeds and chop into small pieces. Heat the butter and sweat the onion, then add the herbs and sauté briefly. Add the tomato purée and brown gently. Finally add the tomatoes and sauté stirring continuously. Pour in the white wine and allow it to reduce.

Pour in the cream and water, and add the sugar, sea salt and pepper to taste. Leave to simmer over a low heat for 20 minutes.

Then add the aubergines and simmer for a further 3 minutes.

Our tip:

The aubergines can be sprinkled with salt several hours in advance. Tomatoes ripened in the sun don't need to be plunged into hot water before removing the skins. If you're in a hurry, tinned tomatoes can be used.

Sweet and Sour Pumpkin

western vegetables meet eastern spices (LG)

serves 4

500 g pumpkin (peeled and seeded)
1 red pepper
1 carrot
1 medium leek
¼ fresh pineapple
20 g butter
1 medium onion, finely chopped
1 teaspoon cornflour

Sauce:
2 tablespoons sesame oil
4 tablespoons soy sauce
4 tablespoons brown sugar
50 ml cider vinegar
1 tablespoon tomato purée
sea salt
400 ml water

Cut the pumpkin into 1 cm cubes, the pepper and carrot into narrow strips, and the leek into thin rings. Dice the pineapple. Mix all the sauce ingredients together in a bowl and set aside.

Heat the butter and sweat the onion. Add the pumpkin and other vegetables, and sauté briefly. Add the sauce, cover, and cook till tender.

Lastly, add the pineapple, bring to the boil, and thicken slightly with corn flour.

Our tip:
There are different kinds of sesame oil, and some are stronger than others. The stronger the flavour, the less oil is required – the sesame flavour could otherwise become too dominant.

Masaman Thai Curry

a particular favourite of mine (Rolf Hiltl) (VG)

serves 4

400 g potatoes
1 medium aubergine
1 red pepper
1 green pepper
1 onion
100 ml groundnut oil
1–2 tablespoons red
Masaman curry paste
600 ml water
1 tablespoon soy extract
1 tablespoon lemon juice
2 tablespoons brown sugar
600 ml coconut milk (tin)
1 teaspoon corn flour
1 apple
a handful unsalted
peanuts

Peel the potatoes and cut them into 2 cm cubes. Cut the aubergine into 2 cm cubes and the peppers into squares. Peel the onion and cut it into quarters, then halve the quarters.

Heat the groundnut oil and sauté the curry paste. Add the potatoes and sauté a little longer. Cover with water, add seasoning, and cook till the potatoes are just tender. Add the aubergine, peppers, onion and coconut milk. Simmer for about 5 minutes and then thicken with cornflour.

Add slices of unpeeled apple to the curry, cover, and simmer very gently for 5 more minutes. Add the peanuts and serve with basmati rice.

Our tip:

Curry paste is available in specialist Thai shops and stores that carry Indian products. However, curry paste often contains shrimps, which is why all curry our pastes are homemade.

Chicory Piccata

a Milanese dish adapted for vegetable lovers (LOG)

serves 4

4 heads chicory
400 ml milky water
(half milk, half water)
1 bay leaf
2 cloves
pepper
sea salt

3 eggs
200 g parmesan cheese,
grated
paprika to taste
30 g butter
3 tablespoons flour
4 lemon wedges

The previous day: Halve the chicory lengthways and remove the core. Place the chicory halves in a bowl with the milk water, bay leaf, cloves, salt and pepper and leave to soak overnight.

The next day: Pour the contents of the bowl into a pan and cook till the chicory is soft. Drain thoroughly in a sieve or colander, place the chicory halves on a chopping board and press flat.

Mix the eggs, cheese and seasonings. Heat the butter. Turn the chicory halves in the flour, dip them into the egg and cheese mixture, and then fry them on both sides until they are golden brown. Serve with a wedge of lemon.

Our tip:

This dish goes particularly well with tomato spaghetti. You can prepare celery, aubergines and courgettes in the same way. For courgettes and aubergines, omit the overnight soaking and pre-cooking. Salt the aubergine slices, leave them to drain on a rack for 30 minutes and then pat dry.

Vegetables with Chestnuts

hot chestnuts – a typical autumn dish (L)

serves 4

5 salsify roots
600 ml milky water
(half milk, half water)
2 tablespoons lemon juice
sea salt
1 bay leaf
2 cloves
2 medium carrots
20 g butter
1 small onion, finely
chopped
400 g frozen chestnuts
sea salt
½ teaspoon turmeric
a pinch of nutmeg
400 ml water
1 bunch marjoram

Peel the salsify roots under running water and cook in the milky water together with the lemon juice, salt, bay leaf and cloves till just tender but still crisp. Drain and cut into 2 cm lengths. Peel the carrots and cut them into julienne sticks.

Heat the butter and sweat the onion. Add the carrots and (frozen) chestnuts, season and cover with water. Simmer until the chestnuts are soft. This should take about 8 minutes. After 4 minutes add the salsify roots and continue to simmer gently. Sprinkle with chopped marjoram before serving.

For fresh chestnuts, make a cut in the round part of the shell. Briefly place in boiling water. Peel while still hot. If the fine brown skin under the shell cannot be slipped off, return to boiling water for a few more minutes.

Our tip:

This dish tastes delicious with spinach noodles.

Spaghetti with Ramsons Pesto

stimulates mind and body (LG)

serves 4 – 6

60 g fresh ramsons leaves
60 g flat-leaf parsley
a little fresh savory
50 g cashew nuts
sea salt
1 teaspoon brown sugar
50 g fresh goat's cheese
80 g parmesan
200 ml olive oil
500 g spaghetti,
e.g. wholemeal
sea salt
olive oil
freshly grated parmesan

Sort the herbs and pull off the leaves. Chop the cashew nuts coarsely.

Blend the herbs, sea salt, sugar, goat's cheese, parmesan and olive oil in a blender. Add the cashew nuts and blend until the pesto is smooth and creamy.

Cook the spaghetti in plenty of salted boiling water until it is al dente. Turn off the heat. Pour off all but a few tablespoons of water, add a little olive oil and return to the hot plate. Over a low heat stir in 4 – 6 tablespoons of ramsons pesto.

Serve with freshly grated parmesan cheese.

Our tip:

In Switzerland ramsons is sold by the bunch: Look for small, tender leaves as they taste best. Ramsons can, of course, be picked in the forest, but there is a danger of confusing them with the highly poisonous leaves of meadow saffron and lily of the valley. Place any leftover pesto in a screw-top jar and store in the fridge for up to a week. If the pesto is too thick, it can be thinned down with a little hot pasta water.

Cereals
Mushrooms

Sweet Corn and Leek Cakes

a well-matched pair (LOG)

serves 4

350 g sweet corn, freshly
cooked or tinned
1 medium leek
5 eggs
3 tablespoons plain flour
sea salt
freshly milled pepper
30 g butter
a pinch of nutmeg

Thoroughly drain the corn kernels. Finely slice the leek. In a bowl, beat the eggs, flour and seasonings. Sauté the leek in some butter until soft, take the pan off the heat and add the sweet corn. Turn the vegetables into the bowl with the egg mixture. Stir thoroughly.

Preheat a frying-pan, add a little butter and, using a soupspoon, distribute the mixture in the pan (this should make about 12 cakes). Fry the cakes on both sides till golden brown.

Serve with a salad in summer and with noodles and a mushroom sauce in winter.

Our tip:
A dash of beer lifts the mixture. You can prepare it in advance, but the cakes should be freshly fried. To make perfectly round or even heartshaped cakes, place pastry cutters into the frying-pan and fill them with the mixture.

Barley Risotto

an old cereal rediscovered (LG)

serves 4

20 g butter
1 small onion, finely chopped
160 g rolled barley
100 ml white wine
1 bay leaf
2 cloves
1 teaspoon sea salt
freshly milled pepper
400 ml water
2 tablespoons olive oil
3 tablespoons parmesan, grated

Heat the butter and sweat the onions until soft. Add the barley and then pour in the white wine. Finally, add the spices and water, bring to the boil, cover and leave on the lowest heat for one hour. Add olive oil and parmesan cheese to taste, and serve the risotto in deep plates.

Serves four as a side dish or two as a main course.

Our tip:
Serve with piccata or a mushroom ragout with marsala sauce.

Gorgonzola Polenta

sweet corn with a zing! (L)

serves 4

1.2 litres water
2 bay leaves
1 clove
140 g (200 ml) fine corn meal
140 g (200 ml) coarse corn meal
sea salt
pepper
60 g butter
100 g gorgonzola

Place the bay leaves, clove and corn meal in the cold water and bring to the boil. Add sea salt and pepper and simmer, covered, on the lowest heat for about one hour. Fold in slivers of butter and the cheese and leave to draw for a further 10 minutes. Taste for seasoning and serve.

Polenta leftovers can be spread 1 cm thick on a baking sheet, left overnight, and then turned out onto a chopping board. The next day, cut into fingers and fry in butter or olive oil till golden brown.

You could also grill the fingers layered in a baking dish. Cover generously with parmesan and dot with butter – delicious served with salad. This gratin also goes very well with braised veal and carrots.

Our tip:

To vary this dish, you could use feta instead of gorgonzola. The rule of thumb for cooking polenta: use three times as much water as corn meal.

Porcini Ragout
superb with a glass of Barolo (L)

serves 4

400 g fresh porcini mushrooms
4 tomatoes
50 ml olive oil
30 g cooking butter
1 onion, finely chopped
2 cloves garlic, thinly sliced
200 ml white wine
a dash of cognac
200 ml water
sea salt, freshly milled pepper
fresh seasonal herbs (e.g. thyme, basil, oregano, parsley)
a pinch of brown sugar (optional)

Clean and slice the mushrooms. Pour boiling water over the tomatoes, leave for 20 seconds and then immediately plunge them into cold water. Slip off the skins, remove the seeds and cut the tomatoes into small pieces.

Heat the olive oil until it is very hot and fry the mushrooms briefly. Strain, taking care to catch the juices. Heat the cooking butter in the same pan and sweat the onions and garlic. Add the white wine and cognac, allow the liquids to reduce, and then cover with water. Add the tomatoes and mushroom juices. Season, and simmer for about 10 minutes until the sauce thickens.

Add the mushrooms and taste for seasoning. Sprinkle with fresh herbs.

Add sugar if the tomatoes themselves are not sweet enough.

Serve with wide noodles.

Mushroom Ragout with Marsala Sauce

and where's the beef? (LG)

serves 4

200 g mixed wild mushrooms (from the market or picked yourself)
100 g oyster mushrooms
100 g brown button mushrooms
1 tablespoon butter
1 small onion, finely chopped
1 clove garlic, crushed
1 teaspoon tomato purée
1-2 teaspoons flour
100 ml red wine
100 ml marsala
200 ml water
sea salt, pepper

Clean the mushrooms with a soft brush or cloth. It's much better not to wash them because they soak up water and lose their flavour. Cut off any damaged parts. Halve or quarter the larger mushrooms but leave the smaller ones intact.

Heat the butter and sweat the onion and garlic. Add the tomato purée and sauté. Increase the heat and gradually add all the mushrooms and then the flour. Stir-fry until everything turns a nice shade of brown. Add the marsala and red wine, reduce the liquids slightly and then add the water. Simmer gently for about 10 minutes. Season to taste with sea salt and pepper. If the sauce is too thick, add a little water.

Our tip:
Serve with mashed potatoes, barley risotto or noodles.

Mushroom Stroganoff

this dish makes the one-off guest a Hiltl regular (L)

serves 4

250 g brown button mushrooms
150 g shiitake mushrooms (Chinese black mushrooms)
200 g oyster mushrooms
2 small red peppers
2 pickled gherkins
50 ml groundnut oil
1 small onion, finely chopped
sea salt
2 teaspoons mild paprika
2 pinches of chilli powder
150 ml good red wine
100 ml water
200 ml cream
sour cream, optional

Clean and quarter the mushrooms. Remove the tough stems of the shiitake mushrooms. Cut the red peppers and gherkins into strips.

Heat the groundnut oil and sear the mushrooms. Add the peppers, gherkins and onion and sauté. Add the spices and red wine. Allow the liquids to reduce a little.

Pour in the water and cream and cook until the desired consistency is reached. Serve with rice or narrow noodles and a splash of sour cream.

Our tip:

Serve with crusty rösti.

Tofu & Co.

Casimir

a classic dish, newly invented (LOG)

serves 4

½ fresh pineapple
1–2 peaches
5 litchis
50 g clarified butter
250 g sliced Quorn, seitan
or tofu
½ onion, finely chopped
1½ teaspoons madras
curry, mild
1½ teaspoons turmeric
½ teaspoon brown sugar
½ teaspoon ground
coriander
1 tablespoon grated
coconut
100 ml dry white wine
300 ml water
200 ml cream
sea salt
a pinch of white pepper

Generously cut off the skin of the pineapple and discard. Slice the pineapple flesh and then cut the slices into small dice. Briefly dip the peaches into boiling water, then plunge into cold water and slip off the skins. Halve them, remove the stones and cut into wedges. Peel the litchis, halve and stone them.

Heat the clarified butter. Stir-fry the Quorn, seitan or tofu until lightly browned. Add the onions and continue frying.

Add the spices and grated coconut and fry briefly. Pour in the wine and let it reduce. Add the cream, water and fruit. Simmer over a low heat for 7 minutes. Season to taste with sea salt and pepper.

Our tip:

Remove the hard centre of the pineapple slices with a small pastry cutter and then dice the fruit.

Tofu Napolitano

with fresh pasta (V)

serves 4

400 g tofu
3 tablespoons olive oil
a small sprig each of rose-mary, marjoram, oregano, thyme, finely chopped
1 clove garlic, crushed
400 g courgettes
400 g tomatoes
3 tablespoons olive oil
½ onion, finely chopped
1 clove garlic, thinly sliced
40 g tomato purée
200 ml dry white wine
500 ml water
½ teaspoon brown sugar
sea salt
freshly milled pepper
3 tablespoons olive oil

The previous day: Cut the tofu into 1 cm dice. Mix with the olive oil, herbs and garlic. Place in the fridge overnight to develop flavours.

The next day: Cut the courgettes into 2 cm dice. Plunge the tomatoes into boiling water, and then rinse them under cold water. Slip off the skins, halve them, remove seeds and chop into small pieces.

Heat the olive oil. Sweat the onion and garlic, add the tomato purée and sauté. Add the tomatoes, pour in the white wine and reduce. Add the water and season with brown sugar, sea salt and pepper. Simmer over a low heat for 20 minutes.

In the meantime, heat the olive oil. Lightly brown the courgettes, remove, and then stir-fry the diced tofu. Stir into the sauce and simmer for a further 5 minutes.

Züri Geschnetzeltes

not just for Zurich's gourmands (LOG)

serves 4

400 g button mushrooms
2 tablespoons
groundnut oil
600 g sliced tofu, Quorn
or seitan
40 g butter
1 onion, finely chopped
a dash of cognac
200 ml white wine
200 ml milk
100 ml cream
sea salt
1 tablespoon lemon juice
freshly milled pepper

Clean the mushrooms and slice thinly. Heat the groundnut oil, sear the tofu (Quorn or seitan) and set aside.

In the same pan, heat the butter and brown the onion. Add the mushrooms and fry a little longer. Add the white wine and cognac, stirring while the liquid reduces. Add the milk and cream, and continue boiling until the sauce has the correct consistency. Lastly, add the tofu (Quorn or seitan) and season with sea salt, lemon juice and pepper.

Served with rösti (Swiss hash browns) or noodles, this tofu Geschnetzeltes is just as good as Zurich's well-known speciality.

Our tip:

If the sauce is too runny, boil to reduce it; if too thick, add some water.

Sweet and Sour Tofu
tofu Chinese style (VG)

serves 4

500 g tofu
1 small carrot
1 red pepper
2 spring onions
200 g shiitake mushrooms
(Chinese black mushrooms)
1 tablespoon groundnut oil
1 tablespoon sesame oil
300 ml water
3 tablespoons cider
vinegar
2 tablespoons brown sugar
2 tablespoons
tomato purée
soy sauce
1 tablespoon corn flour
300 g freshly diced
pineapple

Marinade:
4 tablespoons sesame oil
50 ml groundnut oil
75 ml soy sauce
4 tablespoons brown sugar
1–2 garlic cloves, chopped
1 walnut-sized piece of
fresh root ginger, finely
chopped
1 tablespoon tomato purée

The previous evening: Mix the marinade ingredients together. Cut the tofu into 1.5 cm cubes, pour the marinade over them, mix well and leave to marinate overnight in the fridge.

The next day: Cut the carrot and pepper into fine strips. Chop the spring onions and cut the green stems into rings. Clean and finely slice the mushrooms.

Remove the tofu from the marinade, reserving the liquids in a small bowl. Heat the groundnut oil and fry the tofu. Remove from the pan and set aside.

Add the sesame oil to the pan and sauté the carrot, pepper, mushrooms and onions. Cover with the marinade, water and vinegar, and season with brown sugar, tomato purée and soy sauce to taste. Bring to the boil and thicken with corn flour. Add the pineapple and tofu and reheat.

Our tip:
This dish is delicious
with basmati rice.

Lime Tofu
our favourite tofu recipe (VG)

serves 4

500 g fresh tofu
1 small carrot
½ leek
1 bunch spring onions
100 ml white wine
50 ml lime juice
100 ml orange juice
1 teaspoon brown sugar
50 ml groundnut oil
1 walnut-sized piece of
fresh root ginger, thinly
sliced
400 ml water
1½ teaspoons corn flour
1 tablespoon soy sauce
2 limes

Marinade:
50 ml soy sauce
juice of 1 lime
1 clove garlic, crushed
1 teaspoon turmeric
sea salt
1 teaspoon mild madras
curry powder

Cut the tofu into cubes of about 1 cm. Mix all the marinade ingredients together, add the tofu and allow to marinate for at least 3 hours.

Cut the carrot and leek into julienne sticks, cut the spring onions – including the green parts – into fine rings. Boil the white wine, orange juice, lime juice and brown sugar until reduced to 50 ml and set aside.

Heat the groundnut oil and sear the tofu, then remove from the pan. In the same pan, briefly sauté the carrots, ginger and leek, add the reduced white wine and the water. Simmer until the vegetables are tender.

Thicken with corn flour. Add the tofu and spring onions. Add sugar and soy sauce to taste.

Serve with basmati rice and lime wedges.

Paprika Geschnetzeltes
perfect with crispy rösti (LOG)

serves 4

60 g clarified butter
600 g sliced Quorn, tofu or seitan
1 onion, thinly sliced
2 cloves garlic, thinly sliced
2 tablespoons paprika
1 teaspoon brown sugar
sea salt
freshly milled papper
a dash of congnac
150 ml dry white wine
300 ml water
300 ml cream
90 g gherkins

Heat the clarified butter and stir-fry the sliced Quorn, tofu or seitan until lightly browned.

Add the onion and garlic and sauté briefly. Season with paprika, brown sugar, sea salt and pepper. Add the white wine and cognac, and allow the liquids to reduce.

Add the water and cream, and simmer over a low heat for 10 minutes. Cut the gherkins into narrow strips and scatter over the dish just before serving.

Indian

Chapati
Indian bread (LG)

makes about 25 chapatis

Indian dough:
500 g white flour
125 g semolina
125 g soft cooking butter
a pinch of sea salt
250 ml lukewarm water

Pour the flour and semolina into a mound on a flat work surface. Add the butter and sea salt, and rub together lightly till the mixture resembles fine breadcrumbs. Make a well in the middle and pour in the water. Make the dough working from the edges inwards, and then knead very thoroughly. Cover and leave to rest for one hour.

This is the basic dough for chapatis (photo on page 104). Roll out the dough about 2 mm thick and cut out rounds approximately 7 cm in diameter. Fry on both sides in a frying-pan. 1 kg of dough should make about 25 chapatis.

Kachari

Indian style calzones with a spicy filling (LOG)

makes about 20 kacharis

one quantity Indian dough (recipe p. 106)

Filling:
1 medium red pepper
2 tablespoons groundnut oil
1 teaspoon white mustard seeds
1 teaspoon cumin seeds
200 g frozen peas
1 teaspoon ground coriander
1 teaspoon garam masala
1 teaspoon brown sugar
sea salt
1 teaspoon hot curry powder
a small pinch of asafoetida

1 egg yolk or water for glazing

Thoroughly re-knead the chapati dough, then roll out about 2 mm thick and cut out circles with a diameter of 8 cm.

For the filling, chop the pepper very finely. Sauté the mustard and cumin seeds in sesame oil, add the peppers, peas, and the remaining spices and crush the ingredients in the pan with a fork. If the mixture becomes very dry, add a dash of water.

Place a tablespoon of filling in the centre of each dough circle. Leave an edge of at least 1.5 cm and brush with egg yolk. Fold the pastry to form calzone and press the edges together firmly.

Deep-fry the calzone or bake them at 190° C in a preheated oven for about 15 minutes.

Our tip:
You can also make these kacharis in advance, as they freeze well. Place the frozen kacharis on a tray and bake in a preheated oven for 30 minutes.

Jaffna Okras

hot lady's fingers (V)

serves 4

1 red pepper
3 tablespoons soy oil
½ teaspoon ground cumin
¼ teaspoon fennel seeds
½ teaspoon black
mustard seeds
¼ teaspoon fenugreek
seeds
2 onions, cut into rings
1 clove garlic, thinly sliced
1 tablespoon tomato
purée
1 piece root ginger, finely
chopped
1 teaspoon paprika
1 teaspoon Jaffna curry
1 tablespoon tamarind
paste
sea salt
400 ml water
400 ml coconut milk (tin)
700 g okras (lady's fingers,
gumbo, bhindi)
3 tablespoons soy oil
a little fresh coriander

Halve the pepper, deseed it and cut into 1 cm squares.

Heat the soy oil. Sauté the ground cumin, fennel seeds, mustard seeds and fenugreek seeds until they give off a spicy smell. Add the pepper, onions and garlic and sauté for 8 minutes. Mix in the tomato purée and the ginger. Season with paprika, curry, tamarind paste and salt. Pour in the coconut milk and water and simmer over a low heat for 15 minutes. Blend the sauce.

In the meantime, prepare the okras and make a fresh cut at the end of their stems.

Heat the soy oil in a frying pan, add the okras and a little sea salt, and fry till they are golden brown. Remove and add to the sauce. If necessary, add a little more sea salt. Just before serving, sprinkle with the coriander. Basmati rice makes a good side dish.

Our tip:

Okras grow throughout the world provided it is hot. When young, the pods are eaten as a vegetable. Ripe okras are dried and processed; the resulting powder is used as seasoning. The pods, which are 5 – 10 cm long, vary in colour from a rich green to a yellowish green, but their ridges should not be brown or black. During cooking, they secrete a gelatinous substance which serves as a natural thickener for sauces. If this is not required, the okras are treated with lemon juice and salt before cooking.

Ravaya

a recipe handed down by my grandmother, Margrith Hiltl (V)

serves 4

2 small aubergines
1 medium courgette
2 red peppers
1 small cauliflower
50 ml groundnut oil
2 teaspoons turmeric
a generous pinch of chilli
powder
2 teaspoons ground
coriander
2 teaspoons hot curry
powder
a pinch of asafoetida
approx. 400 ml water
200 g frozen peas
sea salt
2 tablespoons grated
coconut

Cut the aubergines, courgette into cubes and the peppers into squares of roughly the same size. Break the cauliflower into medium-sized florets.
Warm the groundnut oil and stir in the spices. First, add the cauliflower, pour in the water, cover, and simmer gently for about 5 minutes. Then add the diced courgette, aubergines and peppers. The vegetables should remain crisp. Finally, add the peas, cook briefly, and season to taste. Sprinkle with grated coconut before serving.
Serve with basmati rice and either mango and apple chutney or orange pickles.

Curried Eggs from Southern India

the hit among our Indian buffet dishes (O)

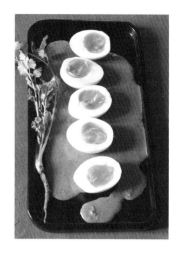

serves 4 – 6

8 fresh eggs
1 large tomato
3 tablespoons soy oil
5 curry leaves, fresh or
dried
½ teaspoon cumin seeds
½ teaspoon black
mustard seeds
1 tablespoon tomato
purée
1 small onion, sliced
1 teaspoon turmeric
1½ teaspoons chilli powder
½ teaspoon fresh root
ginger, chopped
1-2 cloves garlic,
thinly sliced
sea salt
½ tablespoon tamarind
paste
½ tablespoon ground
coriander
2 tablespoons brown sugar
300 ml water
1 tablespoon lemon juice
400 ml coconut milk (tin)
2 tablespoons ground
hazelnuts
a little fresh coriander,
finely chopped

Hard-boil the eggs for 10 minutes, drain. Plunge into cold water, peel, and set aside covered.

Plunge the tomatoes into boiling water, and then rinse them under cold water. Slip off the skins, halve them, remove seeds and cut into small dice. Heat the soy oil and sauté curry leaves, cumin and mustard seeds for 2 minutes. Add the tomato purée and sauté. Finally add the onion slices and sauté for a further 5 minutes.

Mix the remaining ingredients – except the coconut milk, hazelnuts and coriander – add to the pan and sauté for 1 minute.

Add the tomatoes, the coconut milk and the hazelnuts and simmer over a low heat for 20 minutes. Blend the sauce.

Just before serving, halve the eggs and arrange with the cut side up. Pour the sauce over and around the eggs and sprinkle with coriander.

Our tip:

Tamarindus indica plays an important part in Asian cooking. The flesh of the fruit is very fibrous, full of hard seeds and has a sour taste. Tamarind is available as pressed pulp or in liquid form. It gives curries their unique flavour, makes dishes spicier and is used as a softening agent in marinades. It is stocked in Asian speciality stores.

Indian Snake Beans

they're quite harmless . . . (V)

serves 4

450 g snake beans
sea salt
2–3 tomatoes
3 tablespoons sesame oil
(gingelly or gingili)
1½ teaspoons black
mustard seeds
½ teaspoon fenugreek
seeds
½ stick cinnamon
2 cloves
3 tablespoons grated
coconut
1 teaspoon fennel seeds
1 tablespoon tomato
purée
2 teaspoons turmeric
1 tablespoon ground
coriander
½ teaspoon chilli powder
1 teaspoon ground cumin
1 tablespoon brown sugar
500 ml water

Cut the beans into 4 cm lengths. Cook in boiling salted water until just tender, drain, refresh and set aside.

Plunge the tomatoes into boiling water, and then rinse them under cold water. Slip off the skins, halve them, remove seeds and cut into small pieces. Heat the sesame oil and sauté the spices from mustard seeds to cloves until they open and smell spicy. Add the grated coconut, fennel seeds and tomato purée and sauté briefly.

Stir in the turmeric and the coriander, chilli and ground cumin and also the brown sugar. Add the tomatoes and water, and simmer over a low heat for 20 minutes. Remove the cinnamon stick and the cloves. Blend the sauce and season with sea salt. Add the beans and reheat briefly. Serve with rice.

Our tip:

Sesame oil tastes nutty and aromatic. It is cold-pressed, rich in polyunsaturated fats and has good storage properties. There are two qualities of sesame oil: The light, golden sesame oil from India, also called gingelly or gingili, is neutral in flavour and ideal for frying and cooking. It is available in Indian speciality stores. The amber coloured oil has a more pungent taste. It is made of roasted seeds and comes from China, Japan and Korea. This quality should not be strongly heated, but be used for flavouring and marinating. It is widely available.

Indian Snake Beans

Basmati Rice

a delicious, aromatic side dish (V)

serves 4

320 g basmati rice
1 tablespoon
groundnut oil
½ cinnamon stick
2 cloves
1 bay leaf
3 whole cardamom
pods
600 ml water
sea salt

Fry the cinnamon, cloves, bay leaf and cardamom pods in the groundnut oil. Add the water, some salt, and bring to the boil.

Put the rice in a sieve, rinse with cold water and pour into the boiling water. Cover, bring back to the boil, turn off the heat and leave to draw for 15 minutes. If you have an induction or gas cooker, simply simmer over the lowest heat for 15 minutes.

Before serving, remove the spices and loosen the rice with a fork.

Lemon Rice

a refreshing accompaniment for hot curries (V)

serves 4

320 g basmati rice
2 tablespoons soy oil
1 teaspoon black mustard seeds
2 cloves
5 curry leaves
½ teaspoon turmeric
1 lemon, juice and zest
sea salt
600 ml water
1 handful soaked sultanas
2 tablespoons cashew nuts or peanuts

Sauté the mustard seeds, cloves, curry leaves and turmeric in the soy oil for 1 minute. Add the lemon juice and zests, water and sea salt and bring to the boil.

Put the rice in a sieve, rinse with cold water and pour into the boiling water. Add the sultanas, cover, bring back to the boil, turn off the heat and leave to draw for 15 minutes. If you have an induction or gas cooker, simply simmer over the lowest heat for 15 minutes.

Before serving, add the roasted cashew nuts or peanuts, and loosen the rice with a fork.

Dushin Rothli
spicy courgette cakes (LG)

serves 4

*1 large courgette,
about 350 g
½ teaspoon sea salt
2 tablespoons yellow
pea flour
2 tablespoon wholemeal
flour
a pinch of ground nutmeg
1 teaspoon cumin seeds
a small pinch of
asafoetida
2 teaspoons brown sugar
chilli powder, optional
butter or oil for frying*

Grate the courgette coarsely into a bowl. Add the salt, stir carefully, and leave on one side for 1 hour. Using your hands, squeeze the water out of the courgette and transfer to a larger bowl. Add the remaining ingredients and mix thoroughly.

Shape the finished mass into cakes and fry on both sides till golden brown.

Our tip:

We make bite-sized courgette cakes and serve them with other side dishes as a kind of extra. This mixture can easily be prepared a day in advance. You could also use only wholemeal flour, but the yellow pea flour gives the dushin rothli that special flavour.

Vadai

crunchy croquettes from our Indian buffet (V)

makes 20 vadai

300 g yellow split peas
1 teaspoon cumin seeds
1 teaspoon fennel seeds
sea salt
1 twig curry leaves
1 small green chilli,
chopped
1 small onion, chopped

oil for deep frying

The previous day: Soak the split peas overnight in three times their volume of cold water.

The next day: Drain the peas thoroughly. Put one tablespoon of the softened peas on one side and place the rest on a chopping board. Chop these with a large knife until the consistency resembles that of corn meal. If you have a cutter, all the better, you'll save a lot of time!

Mix the finely chopped peas with the remaining ingredients including the whole peas. Using a tea-spoon, form the mixture into walnut-sized balls and place them on a baking sheet lined with baking paper. Heat the oil to 180° C, and deep-fry the balls a few at a time. Served with rice, dal, and coconut chutney, vadai make an excellent, nutritious meal.

Our tip:
You can prepare the vadai in advance and freeze them. Then simply fry the frozen vadai as required. Serve with shrikand (recipe on page 160) as a snack.

Aubergine Curry

a quick dish, good at any time of the year (V)

serves 4

one small green chillis
2 large aubergines
4 medium tomatoes
2 tablespoons
groundnut oil
1 teaspoon cumin seeds
1 small twig curry leaves
2 teaspoons turmeric
a generous pinch of
ground coriander
a pinch of asafoetida
sea salt
300 ml water

Finely chop the chilli. Cut the aubergine into 1.5 cm cubes. Dice the tomato.

Heat the groundnut oil and sauté the cumin seeds. Add the chilli and sauté briefly. Then add the remaining spices, and again sauté briefly. Add the aubergine cubes and cover with water. Simmer for about 5 minutes, add the tomatoes and cook till tender.

Serve with lemon rice and coconut chutney.

Our tip:

Cumin, also sold as jeera, is a common spice in Indian cooking and a basic ingredient in curry powders. It is said to aid the digestion. The pale cumin seeds are aromatic, warm and dry. They should not be confused with caraway seeds – their flavour is quite different. Black cumin seeds have a more pungent flavour.

Coriander Pilau
one of many pilau variations (V)

serves 4

approx. 250 g long grain or basmati rice
2 medium potatoes
2 tablespoons flaked almonds
4 small courgettes
1 large onion
50 ml groundnut oil
a generous pinch of chilli powder
2 teaspoons mild madras curry powder
1 teaspoon turmeric
2 teaspoons ground coriander
1 teaspoon sea salt
1 teaspoon garam masala
200 ml water
50 g frozen peas

Cook the rice in salted water as you would for a side dish and set aside.

Boil the potatoes, peel, and set aside. Without adding any fat, toast the almonds in a non-stick frying-pan and set aside. Cut the courgettes into 5 mm rounds and the onion into rings.

Heat the groundnut oil and gently sweat the onions. Add all the spices and sauté briefly. Add the courgettes and water, stir, and bring to the boil. Simmer for about 3 minutes only, as courgettes don't take long to cook.

Coarsely grate the potatoes into the mixture. Loosen the cooked rice with a fork and add to the mixture together with the peas.

Serve sprinkled with toasted almonds.

Our tip:

This dish is an ideal way of using up leftover rice and potatoes. You can also vary the amount of rice depending on whether you want a rice dish or a vegetable side dish with rice.

South Indian Avival

from Kerala (L)

serves 4

*200 g pumpkin
(peeled and seeded)*
1–2 courgettes
2–3 potatoes
sea salt
3 tablespoons coconut oil
4 curry leaves
1 teaspoon mustard seeds
½ teaspoon cumin seeds
*1 tablespoon chillies,
chopped*
½ cinnamon stick
10 black peppercorns
½ onion, finely chopped
½ teaspoon ground cumin
*1 teaspoon ground
coriander*
1 teaspoon turmeric
½ teaspoon chilli powder
1 tablespoon water
*400 ml coconut milk
(tinned)*
200 ml water
*1 piece fresh root ginger,
finely chopped*
1 teaspoon brown sugar
sea salt
500 g plain yoghurt
a little fresh coriander

Cut the pumpkin and courgettes into 1.5 cm cubes. Peel the potatoes, cut into 1.5 cm cubes and boil in salted water until just tender. Drain thoroughly and set aside.

Heat the coconut oil and sauté the curry leaves, mustard and cumin seeds, chillies, cinnamon stick and peppercorns until the give off a spicy smell. Add the chopped onion and sauté a little longer. Mix the cumin, coriander, chilli and turmeric with the water to make a paste and add to the pan.

Add the coconut milk, water, ginger, brown sugar and sea salt. Simmer over a low heat for 10 minutes. Remove the cinnamon stick and blend the sauce.

Add the pumpkin and the courgettes, and cook until just tender. Add the potatoes and yoghurt. Heat, but do not allow to boil.

Serve sprinkled with the coriander.

Our tip:

Fresh curry leaves are available at Indian grocery stores. They can be deep-frozen to maintain their strong flavour. They can, of course, be dried – but then much of their taste is lost.

Paneer

Indian soft cheese (L)

serves 4–6

1 litre organic whole milk
3 tablespoons cider vinegar
1 tablespoon lemon juice

Heat the milk in a large pan till it starts to rise. Then stir in the vinegar and lemon juice. The milk will curdle (this is the paneer or curds). Line a sieve with a folded cheesecloth and pour in the curdled milk. Then rinse the curds in the sieve under running cold water for about 1 minute. Then hold the ends of the cloth and press out the liquid. Knot or tie the ends together and place the curds in the cloth between two chopping boards. Place weights of roughly 5 kg on the top board (e.g. tinned food) and leave overnight in the fridge. The following day the cheese will be firm enough to slice.

It will keep for up to 4 days in the fridge.

Paneer Makhani
a popular sauce from northern India (L)

serves 4

500 g tomatoes
400 g red peppers
60 g clarified butter
½ teaspoon fenugreek seeds
1 teaspoon cumin seeds
1 onion, cut into rings
1 clove garlic, thinly sliced
70 g tomato purée
½ teaspoon turmeric
½ teaspoon ground cardamom
½ tablespoon paprika
½ teaspoon ground cumin
½ teaspoon garam masala
½ teaspoon ground ginger
½ teaspoon chilli powder
1 tablespoon fenugreek leaves
500 ml water
sea salt
2 tablespoons brown sugar
600 g paneer,
see left-hand page

Plunge the tomatoes into boiling water, and then rinse them under cold water. Slip off the skins, halve them, remove seeds and cut into small pieces. Halve the peppers, remove the seeds and cut into 1 cm squares.

Heat the butter and sauté the fenugreek and cumin seeds. Add the onion rings and garlic and sauté briefly. Stir in the tomato purée.

Stir in the remaining spices and the fenugreek leaves, mix well and sauté until the mixture smells spicy.

Add the tomatoes and water and simmer over a low heat for 30 minutes. Blend the sauce and season with sea salt and brown sugar. Add the peppers and simmer for a further 10 minutes.

Cut the paneer into 1 cm cubes, add to the sauce and heat, but do not boil.

Basmati rice makes a good side dish.

Our tip:
If you prefer a hotter sauce, add more chilli powder. However, it becomes hotter the longer it cooks, so it is worth adding only a little extra chilli at a time.

Bengali Vegetables

White Curry

Rajma

Rajma
enjoy this dish in style with an Indian beer (V)

serves 4

200 g red kidney beans
1 small aubergine
5 tomatoes
2 tablespoons groundnut oil
1 small onion, finely chopped
1 teaspoon garam masala
a pinch of chilli powder
a small piece of fresh root ginger, thinly sliced
2 teaspoons ground coriander
1 teaspoon turmeric
100 ml water
sea salt
1 bunch fresh coriander

The previous day: Pick over and wash the beans and soak them overnight in three times their volume of water.

The next day: Cook the beans in this water, drain, and set aside.

Dice the aubergine and tomatoes. Heat the groundnut oil and sweat the onions. Add all the spices and the aubergine. Cover with water and simmer until tender.

Add the cooked beans and the diced tomatoes. If necessary, add more water. Season with sea salt. Bring back to the boil briefly and serve sprinkled with freshly chopped coriander.

Our tip:
If the tomatoes are a little sour, add a pinch of sugar. Serve with basmati rice and sour cream.

Bengali Vegetables
a gentle tiger elegantly spiced (V)

serves 4

200 g pumpkin
(peeled and seeded)
1 medium courgette
1 small aubergine
1 small green chilli
1 tablespoon
groundnut oil
2 teaspoons white
mustard seeds
2 teaspoons fenugreek
seeds
2 teaspoons cumin seeds
1 teaspoon fennel seeds
400 ml water
2 teaspoons sea salt
1 tablespoon brown sugar
80 g french beans
1 teaspoon corn flour
80 g peas, fresh or frozen

Cut the pumpkin, courgette and aubergine into 1.5 cm cubes. Finely chop the chilli.

Heat the groundnut oil and gently fry the mustard, fenugreek, cumin and fennel seeds until they smell aromatic. Add the chilli and pumpkin, sauté briefly, then add the water, salt and sugar, and bring to the boil. After 3 to 5 minutes add the courgette, aubergine and beans. Simmer until the vegetables are tender.

Add corn flour to thicken as desired. Lastly, add the peas and heat through.

Our tip:

You can substitute carrots for the pumpkin. Serve with basmati rice and some mango and apple chutney.

White Curry
cooked with milk (L)

serves 4

1 small green chilli
1 small leek
3 large carrots
200 ml milk
2 tablespoons
groundnut oil
1 medium onion, cut into
rings
1 twig curry leaves
1 teaspoon black mustard
seeds
1 teaspoon fennel seeds
½ teaspoon cumin seeds
1 tablespoon brown sugar
sea salt
1 teaspoon turmeric
100–200 ml water

Finely chop the chilli. Cut the leek into fine strips. Peel the carrots and cut into 5 mm slices. Boil the milk in a pan to reduce it to half its volume.

Heat the groundnut oil and sauté the onions, chilli, mustard seeds, fennel seeds, curry leaves and cumin until the onions are soft but not brown. Add the leek, carrots, and the remaining spices. Cover with water, mix well and, stirring occasionally, cook until the vegetables are tender but still crisp.

Lastly, pour in the milk. Reheat but do not boil – otherwise the milk will curdle.

Serve with coconut chutney and basmati rice.

Dal

red lentil purée (V)

serves 4

1 tablespoon groundnut oil
2 teaspoons cumin seeds
1 teaspoon fennel seeds
1 teaspoon black mustard seeds
1 small onion, sliced
1 clove garlic, crushed
1 small green chilli, finely chopped
1 small twig curry leaves
160 g red lentils
800 ml water
a small pinch of chilli powder
1 teaspoon turmeric
2 teaspoons garam masala
1 teaspoon hot curry powder
sea salt

Heat the groundnut oil and brown the cumin and fennel seeds. Add the mustard seeds, onion, garlic, chilli and curry leaves, and sauté.
Add the lentils and cover with water. Finally, add the remaining spices and simmer gently for about 90 minutes, stirring occasionally.
Dal goes with any Indian dish including basmati rice.

Our tip:

We serve this dish as a salad by thinning it with a little water and adding freshly chopped coriander. Add more water, and you could serve it as a warm soup. With less water and chilled, it makes an excellent dip for fresh vegetables. You can prepare dal in advance - it keeps for about three days.

Arab

Arab Bamja
the new Hiltl hit (V)

serves 4

400 g okras (lady's fingers, gumbo, bhindi)
300 g tomatoes
3 tablespoons olive oil
½ onion, finely chopped
2 cloves garlic, thinly sliced
1 tablespoon tomato purée
1 teaspoon brown sugar
1 teaspoon ground ginger
a pinch of saffron
1 teaspoon cumin seeds
1 teaspoon ground coriander
sea salt
freshly milled pepper
500 ml water
3 tablespoons olive oil

Prepare the okras and make a fresh cut at the end of their stems. Plunge the tomatoes into boiling water, and then rinse them under cold water. Slip off the skins, halve them, remove seeds and cut into small pieces. Heat the olive oil and sweat the onion and garlic for 5 minutes. Add the tomato purée and the sugar. Sauté for 2 minutes.

Add the spices, cover with water and simmer gently over a low heat for 30 minutes.

Add the tomatoes and continue cooking for a further 5 minutes, then take the pan off the heat.

In a frying pan, heat the olive oil, add the salt and stir-fry the okras until they are lightly browned. Add to the sauce and bring to the boil briefly.

Serve with rice, brown bread or, as in North Africa, with the traditional warm flat bread.

Our tip:
If you'd like this dish a little hotter, you could use harissa or sambal oelek.

Couscous Marrakech

by our chef Rachid Amersid (V)

serves 4

70 g chickpeas
1 medium courgette
1 red pepper
150 g pumpkin (peeled and seeded)
1 large potato, peeled
3 tablespoons olive oil
½ onion, chopped
1 clove garlic, chopped
1 tablespoon tomato purée
15 saffron threads
1 teaspoon ground ginger
¼ teaspoon cinnamon
1 teaspoon ground cumin
1 teaspoon ground coriander
1 teaspoon paprika
700–800 ml water
sea salt
freshly milled pepper
a little fresh coriander or flat-leaf parsley

The previous day: Wash the chickpeas and soak them overnight in three times their volume of cold water.

The next day: Bring the chickpeas to the boil in their soaking water and cook till soft. Drain and set aside.

Cut the vegetables into 3 cm cubes and the potatoes into 2 cm cubes.

Heat the olive oil and sweat the onion and garlic. Add the tomato purée and sauté.

Add the spices and sauté until they give off a rich aroma. Pour in the water and simmer for 10 minutes. Blend the sauce.

Add the potatoes and cook till they are just tender, then add the courgette, pepper and pumpkin and simmer over a low heat until tender.

Just before serving, add the cooked chickpeas and season with sea salt and pepper. Sprinkle with coriander or parsley leaves. Serve with couscous.

Our tip:

Always soak saffron threads in a little water before using so that they can develop their rich aroma and strong colour.

Couscous

a quick and easy dish (VG)

280 g couscous
400 ml water
sea salt
2 pinches of ground cumin

Pour the couscous into a bowl. Mix with water, sea salt and cumin. Place in the middle of the oven preheated to 100°C for 20 minutes. Loosen with a fork before serving.

Lebanese Badingal
interesting and exotic (V)

serves 4

125 g chickpeas
500 g aubergines
1 teaspoon sea salt
olive oil for frying
350 g tomatoes,
e.g. San Marzano
3 tablespoons olive oil
1 medium onion, cut into
small wedges
1 clove garlic, thinly sliced
½ teaspoon cumin seeds
2 tablespoons tomato
purée
1 small cinnamon stick
1 teaspoon ground
coriander
¼ teaspoon chilli powder
1 teaspoon brown sugar
sea salt
freshly milled pepper
700 ml water
a few drops of orange
blossom water
3–4 tablespoons pine
nuts, roasted

The previous day: Wash the chickpeas and soak them overnight in three times their volume of cold water.

The next day: Bring the chickpeas to the boil in their soaking water and cook till soft. Drain and set aside.

Cut the aubergines into 1.5 cm cubes, mix with the sea salt and place in a sieve or colander for 20 minutes. Pat dry with kitchen paper. Heat the olive oil and stir-fry the aubergines until they are lightly browned. Remove and set aside.

Plunge the tomatoes into boiling water, and then rinse them under cold water. Slip off the skins, halve them, remove seeds and cut into small pieces. Slowly heat the olive oil together with the onion, garlic and cumin seeds, stirring all the time. Sauté over a low heat until they are soft and transparent. Add the tomatoes and tomato purée and sauté a little longer. Add the cinnamon stick, the other spices and the water and simmer for 15 minutes. Add the chickpeas and aubergines and simmer for 5 minutes.

Season with orange blossom water and, before serving, sprinkle pine nuts over the dish.

Our tip:
Serve with rice and peppermint yoghurt: to make this, mix a generous amount of finely chopped mint into plain yoghurt and season with sea salt and pepper. Spices develop a more intense flavour if they are first roasted in a pan without oil; the spices should be individually roasted.

Sauces
Chutneys

Lime Salad Sauce
light and refreshing (V)

serves 6–8

100 g flat-leaf parsley
250 ml lime juice, freshly
squeezed
1 lime, grated peel
1 teaspoon ground cumin
1 teaspoon ground
cardamom
1 level tablespoon sea salt
1–2 tablespoons brown
sugar
1–2 cloves garlic, crushed
70 ml cider vinegar
300 ml olive oil

Remove the parsley leaves from the stems. Place the leaves and all the other ingredients except the olive oil in a mixer and blend thoroughly. Then very gradually add the olive oil, mixing all the time.

Our tip:

Prepared without garlic, this sauce can be poured into a bottle and kept in the fridge for about 10 days. It goes well with all leaf salads, and particularly with fresh asparagus.

Ginger Raita

makes an excellent accompaniment for Indian curries (L)

serves 4

1 piece cucumber,
about 3–4 cm
1 tomato
1 tablespoon fresh root
ginger
360 g yoghurt
1 teaspoon mustard seeds
a few fresh coriander
leaves
sea salt
brown sugar

Cut all the vegetables into tiny dice (do not peel the cucumber). Grate the ginger very finely. Mix the vegetables and ginger into the yoghurt. Grind the mustard seeds in a pepper mill – or use a mortar and pestle or rolling pin to crush them – and add to the mixture. Add the finely snipped coriander leaves.
Season to taste with sea salt and brown sugar.

Our tip:
Fresh root ginger can be quite hot. Make the sauce with different amounts of ginger and you'll soon know how much to use.

Mayonnaise

a quick mayonnaise
that always works (O)

serves 8

200 ml sunflower oil
1 fresh egg
½ teaspoon mustard
sea salt
a little lemon juice

Fill the sunflower oil, egg and mustard into a tall mixing glass.

With a wand mixer (use the beater) mix for 30 seconds holding the wand steady. Then continue mixing drawing the wand up and down. It takes just one minute to make the mayonnaise. Season with sea salt and lemon juice.

Our tip:

The ingredients must all have the same temperature: Take the egg out of the fridge early enough. The mayonnaise can also be made with 100 ml each of sunflower oil and olive oil.

Almonaise

a mayonnaise
without eggs (V)

serves 8

200 ml sunflower oil
100 ml cold water
1 tablespoon vinegar
1 teaspoon mustard
1 tablespoon almond
purée
sea salt

Put all the ingredients – except the sea salt – into a tall mixing glass.

With a wand mixer (use the beater) mix for 30 seconds holding the wand steady. Then continue mixing drawing the wand up and down. It takes just one minute to make the almonaise. Season with sea salt.

Our tip:

The almonaise is not only made without eggs, it is also low calorie because of the amount of water used. Almond purée is available in health food stores. Always stir well before use.

Date Chutney

a subtly flavoured chutney from southern India (V)

serves 4

100 g dates
1 large onion,
finely chopped
1 small green chilli, finely
chopped
a little fresh coriander,
finely chopped
2 teaspoons brown sugar
3 tablespoons lemon juice
½ teaspoon ground cumin
sea salt
1 piece fresh root ginger,
finely chopped
1 tablespoon soy oil
1–2 tablespoons pear
juice concentrate
4 tablespoons tomato
purée
5 tablespoons sultanas

Halve the dates, pit them and cut into fine slices. Place the remaining ingredients into a bowl and mix thoroughly. Stir in the dates. Fill the chutney into a screw jar and store in the fridge.
It will keep for 1–2 weeks.

Our tip:
60 g of pear juice concentrate has the sweetening properties of 100 g sugar. This natural liquid sweetener looks like honey, has a slight caramel flavour and, of course, tastes of pears. It is the traditional sweetener used in gingerbread. It is available in health food stores and in some supermarkets.

Coconut Chutney

a recipe from southern India (L)

serves 4

1 green chilli, finely chopped
1 small onion, finely chopped
1 bunch curry leaves
approx. 160 ml milk
a dash of lemon juice
a pinch of sea salt
a pinch of brown sugar
100 g grated coconut

Place all the ingredients – except the grated coconut – together with 100 ml of the milk into a blender. Blend thoroughly. Add the coconut and blend again briefly. Pour into a bowl and gradually add the remaining milk until the desired consistency is reached.

Our tip:

The chutney should not be too runny. You can store it in the fridge for up to two days.

Tahini

serve with olive bread
or on crostini toast (L)

serves 4 (as an entrée)

200 g chickpeas, dried, or 430 g cooked	*1 teaspoon lemon juice*
	sea salt
100 g sesame paste	*1 teaspoon mild paprika*
360 g yoghurt	*1 bunch flat-leaf parsley,*
1 clove garlic, finely	*chopped*
chopped	*2 tablespoons olive oil*

The previous day: Pick over the chickpeas (in case of small stones) and wash thoroughly. Soak overnight in three times their volume of water.

The next day: Cook the chickpeas in the same water until they are very soft, and drain well. With a fork, mash the chickpeas into a purée, then add the remaining ingredients and season to taste.

Our tip:

The tahini has more zip
if you add a little Tabasco
or harissa.

Shrikand

curd cheese
with saffron (L)

serves 4

500 g low-fat curd cheese
60 g brown sugar
a generous pinch of saffron
some milk

Mix all the ingredients together thoroughly. If the curd cheese is very firm, add some more milk.

An excellent contrast to spicy Indian foods.

Our tip:

This saffron curd cheese also makes a good dessert. Serve with toasted almonds.

Madras Sauce

we kept this recipe a strictly guarded secret for many years (V)

makes 1 litre

3 large onions
100 ml groundnut oil
1 tablespoon tomato purée
3 tablespoons grated coconut
3 teaspoons mild madras curry powder
2 tablespoons hot madras curry powder

½ teaspoon ground cardamom
1 teaspoon ground coriander
a pinch of chilli powder
1 tablespoon brown sugar
sea salt
1 litre water

Cut the onions into rings. Heat the groundnut oil and sweat the onions for about 10 minutes till they are soft but not brown. Add the tomato purée, grated coconut, spices, sugar and salt. Cover with water and simmer uncovered for at least one hour, stirring occasionally.

Place in a blender and purée until smooth. Taste and season with more salt and chilli powder if desired.

Our tip:

You can prepare this sauce in advance. It keeps in the fridge for several days. You can also freeze it in portions. Thinned down with stock and served with fresh croutons it makes a tasty curried onion soup.

Cress Salad Dressing

light, and low on calories (L)

makes 200 ml

1 teaspoon Dijon mustard
5 drops Tabasco
50 ml lemon juice
1 small carton cress
180 g yoghurt
1 bunch parsley

1 teaspoon sea salt
a pinch of brown sugar

Purée all the ingredients in a blender.
Please note: This sauce must always be prepared just before serving, otherwise it loses its attractive shade of green.
Ideal for summer leaf salads.

You can also purchase these sauces and chutneys in our restaurant.

Desserts

Brownies
the recipe our regular guests swear by (LOG)

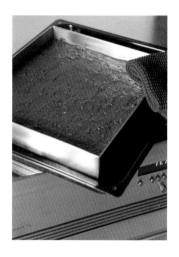

makes 25
(30 x 27 cm baking tin)

360 g butter
490 g vanilla couverture,
grated (dark couverture)
5 organic eggs, more
than 55 g
a pinch of salt
540 g brown sugar
½ teaspoon vanilla sugar
450 g shelled walnuts
360 g plain flour
butter for the tin

Melt the butter and vanilla couverture (or dark cooking chocolate) in a small pan on the lowest heat.

Beat the eggs, salt, sugar and vanilla sugar till they are frothy.

Carefully fold the egg mixture into the butter-chocolate mixture. Fold in the flour and the nuts. Preheat the oven to 180° C.

Generously butter the baking tin. Place the brownie mixture into the tin and spread smoothly. Bake for about 22 minutes in the lower third of the oven (about 4 minutes less in a convection oven).

Leave to cool and then cut into 4 cm squares.

Our tip:
Brownies can be stored in a tin for several days.

Mango Ice Cream
a real favourite in our restaurant (LO)

makes 500 ml

*4–6 very ripe
mangoes
2 tablespoons lemon
juice
20 g brown sugar,
depending on how
sweet the mangoes are
2 egg whites
100 ml cream*

Peel the mangoes, cut the flesh away from the stone, place in a blender and purée until smooth. This should give you 400 g fairly runny mango puree. Beat the egg whites lightly with a fork. Mix all the ingredients thoroughly and place in the freezer. After 30 minutes, stir the mixture thoroughly and return it to the freezer. Stir again thoroughly after 45 minutes and after 60 minutes. Then allow the ice-cream to freeze completely.

Without the cream, you'd make a mango sorbet.

Our tip:

If you own an ice-cream maker, you can save yourself the stirring, with the added bonus of producing even lighter ice cream.

Nut Salad

there's a taste of Christmas about this salad (L)

serves 4

200 g shelled walnuts
50 g dried dates
100 g dried figs
50 g dried bananas
175 g fresh pineapple
pieces
1 tablespoon sultanas
2–3 apples, about 250 g
1 tablespoon lemon juice
350 ml cream

Use a cutter or knife to coarsely chop the nuts, dates, figs, bananas. Add the sultanas and pineapple. Wash and coarsely grate the apple, leaving the peel on. Immediately mix with the lemon juice.

Whip the cream, and mix all the ingredients together. Serve immediately.

Easter Cake

a real Hiltl speciality (LOG)

makes 2 cakes of 18 cm Ø
(about 12 pieces)

Rice for the filling:
180 rice, Vialone
200 ml water
600 ml milk
2 teaspoons brown sugar
a pinch of sea salt

Shortcrust pastry:
200 g plain flour
100 g softened butter
a small pinch of sea salt
1 egg
1–2 teaspoons sugar

Filling:
100 g marzipan
40 g brown sugar
50 g butter
a generous pinch of grated
lemon peel
approx. 1 tablespoon
water
2 eggs
140 ml cream
40 g sultanas

butter for greasing the tin

Bring the rice to a boil in 200 ml water. Add the milk and simmer on the lowest possible heat for about an hour until the rice is soft, adding more water if required. Then add the sugar and salt. Allow to cool down completely.

For the pastry, rub the butter and flour between your fingers until fine crumbs are formed. Add the salt, egg and sugar, and mix until smooth. If the pastry is too crumbly, add a few drops of water. Form the pastry into a ball, wrap it in foil, and leave to rest in the fridge for at least one hour or over-night.

For the filling, mix the marzipan, sugar, butter, grated lemon peel, water and eggs together for about 15 minutes. Stir in the rice. Whip the cream and stir into the mixture.

Preheat the oven to 170° C. Halve the pastry, and roll out each half into circles approximately 20 cm in diameter. Place the pastry in two 18 cm baking tins and prick closely with a fork. Sprinkle the sultanas over the pastry and then spread the filling over them. Bake in the lower third of the oven for about 25 minutes.

Our tip:
This cake tastes best when freshly baked. You can, however, prepare the pastry in advance and freeze it.

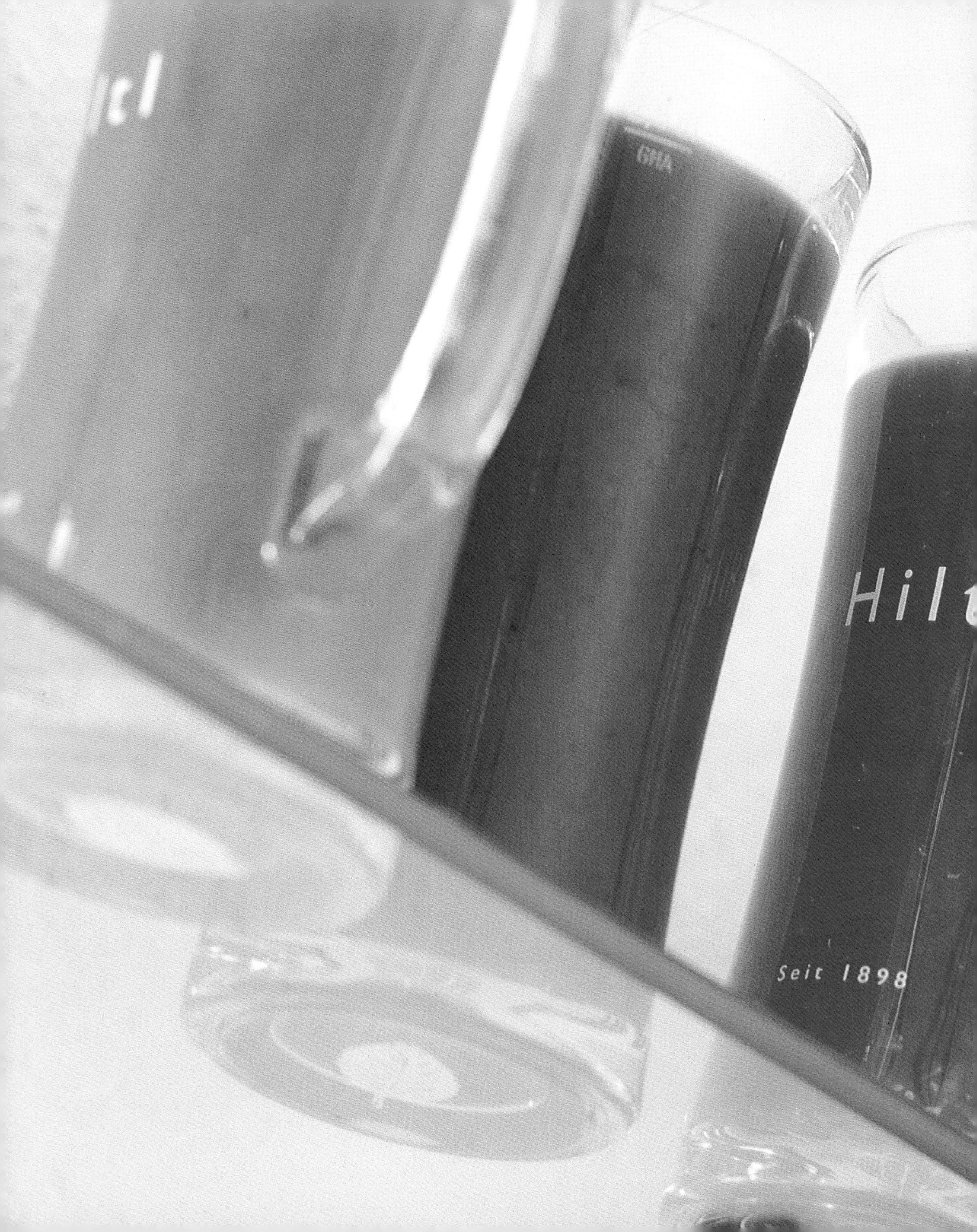
GHA
Hilt
Seit 1898

Drinks

The Call of Spring (L)

serves 2 (600-700 ml)

400 ml orange juice
180 g Bifidus yoghurt
100 ml sea-buckthorn syrup

Use a hand whisk to mix thoroughly.

Indian Juice (V)

serves 2 (700 ml)

2 very ripe mangoes
200 ml orange juice
1 tablespoon lemon juice
a pinch of garam masala

Peel the mangoes and cut the flesh away from the stone. Either use a wand mixer or place in a blender together with the other ingredients and liquidise. Strain through a sieve if desired.

Apricotine (V)

serves 2 (600 ml)

½ small apple
4 apricots
1 handful raspberries
300 ml orange juice
100 ml water

Chop the apples and apricots. Either use a wand mixer or place in a blender together with the other ingredients and liquidise. Don't strain, unless the raspberry seeds bother you!

Autumn Juice (V)

serves 2 (600 ml)

½ lemon, juice
½ apple
400 g white grapes,
e.g. Regina
80 g blueberries (about 4 table-spoons)
200 ml water

Wash and core the apple, wash the blueberries and grapes. Coarsely chop all the ingredients, liquidise and strain through a sieve.

Santa's Juice (V)

serves 2 (500-600 ml)

300 ml orange juice
2 tangerines
3 dates, stoned and chopped
a pinch of ground cinnamon

Liquidise all the ingredients and strain through a sieve.

Masala Coffee (L)

serves one

approx. 20 g dark bitter chocolate (1 row)
150 ml strong black coffee
100 ml milk
1–2 tablespoons whipped cream
a pinch of garam masala
chocolate powder
sugar as desired

Melt the chocolate in a pan with the coffee but do not boil. Pour into a large glass. Heat the milk and add it to the glass. Mix well. Spoon the whipped cream on top, sprinkle with garam masala and chocolate powder, and serve hot.

Melo-Melo (V)

serves 2 (600 ml)

300 ml orange juice
1 small cantaloupe or honeydew
melon
½ apple

Finely chop the apple and melon. Place all the ingredients in a blender and liquidise.

Our tip:

With a dash of rosewater this drink has an elegant Indian flavour.

Tropical (V)

serves 2 (500 ml)

300 ml orange juice
4 passion fruit
1 guava
2 slices fresh pineapple

Finely chop all the ingredients, liquidise, and strain through a sieve.

Various Vegetarians

All vegetarians can eat a really enjoyable meat at the Hiltl.

Pesco/pollo vegetarians
Also known as semi-vegetarians. Their food is mainly vegetarian but with a few exceptions. Thus they eat fish and poultry. More than 90 percent of Hiltl's guests are semi-vegetarians.

Lacto-ovo vegetarians
They eat nothing made of animals that have been slaughtered, i.e. no sausage, no poultry, no fish, no gelatine, etc. The food in the Hiltl restaurant is lacto-ovo vegetarian.

Lacto vegetarians
Like lacto-ovo vegetarians except that they eat no eggs (animal derivative). Eggs are clearly declared (O) in the recipes and in our special menu in the restaurant.

Ovo vegetarians
They eat eggs but no dairy products (animal derivative). Milk products are clearly declared (L) in the recipes and in our special menu in the restaurant.

Vegans
They avoid all animal-based foodstuffs (including animal derivative foods such as milk, dairy products, eggs and honey). They often also reject all animal products in their day-to-day life, such as in their clothing (no leather jackets, shoes, etc.). Vegan dishes are clearly declared (V) in the recipes and in our special menu in the restaurant.

Symbols:
(V) vegan
(L) with dairy products
(O) with eggs
(G) with gluten

Glossary and Comments

Glossary

Since the weights and measures given in this book are metric, we opted for standard British usage with regard to terminology. However, we are aware that terminology differs throughout the English-speaking world and that British and American usage, in particular, can easily lead to confusion. Although certainly not exhaustive, we hope you'll find the short list below helpful.

Aubergine – eggplant
Chillies – chili peppers – chilies
Corn flour – cornstarch
Courgette – zucchini
Fenugreek – methi
Gherkins – pickles
Peppers – bell peppers
Ramsons – wood garlic – bear's garlic
Salsify – oyster plant – vegetable oyster
Snow peas – mangetout – sugar peas
Wholemeal– whole wheat
Yoghurt – yogurt

A dash – a few drops

Season to taste

Instead of rock salt, the Hiltl chefs use sea salt. This delicious salt is also known as *fleur de sel*.

Pepper should always be freshly milled or ground in a pestle and mortar. We don't give any quantities for pepper and salt because that's a matter of individual taste.

In recipes with a high acid content, e.g. vinegar or tomatoes, sugar reduces the acid and brings out the flavour. According to taste, the sugar can be omitted in most of the recipes.

Asafoetida is an Indian spice and tastes of garlic. A little fresh garlic could be used instead.

Conversion basics

The figures below are approximations and intended only to serve as a guide.

Temperature:	100°C ≈ 200°F, 150°C ≈ 300°F, 200°C ≈ 400°F
Volume:	250 ml ≈ 1 cup ≈ 8 fl oz
Mass:	60 g ≈ 2 oz
Length:	5 cm ≈ 2 in

We're Hiltl

as international as our guests

Ana
Iran

Ganesch
Sri Lanka

Hugo
Portugal

Hüseyin
Turkey

Sara
Switzerland

Marielle
France

Nick
Austria

Natalya
Ukraine

Beat
Switzerland

Raul
Spain

Flurina
Switzerland

Katja
Switzerland

Slavica
Serbia

Virat
India

Jana
Germany

Djabba
France

Silvan
Switzerland

Anuschka
Switzerland

Silvija
Serbia

Susanne
Switzerland

Sri
Sri Lanka

Fujia
China

Reza
Afghanistan

Anja
Switzerland

Slavisa
Serbia

Bel
Congo

Barbara
Switzerland

Mario
Germany

Raphaèle
Switzerland

Vera
Serbia

Fatmir
Kosovo

Ahmed
Somalia

Rainer
Switzerland

Sira
Spain

Peter
Switzerland, USA

Julbert
France

Daniel
Switzerland

Lozoyodo
Tibet

Nicole
Switzerland

Léocadie
Congo

Bernadette
Austria

Dani
Austria

Thomas
Ghana

Banu
Turkey

Nevenka
Bosnia

| | Oscar
Switzerland | Brigitte
Switzerland | Tashi
Tibet | Désirée
Switzerland | Asa
Sweden | Miek Nether-
lands, Switzerland | Agung, Indonesia,
Switzerland | Rachid, Morocco,
Switzerland |
| sia | | | | | | | | |

| | Amanda
Switzerland | Rolf
Switzerland | Arnold
Germany | Saleban
Somalia | Adnan
Kosovo | Kamina
Sri Lanka | Andi
Switzerland | Laila
Switzerland |
| bia | | | | | | | | |

| | Helmut
Austria | Azeem, Pakistan,
Switzerland | Yueping
China | Zia
Afghanistan | Erika
Switzerland | Mila
Switzerland | Natascha
Switzerland | Zorica
Serbia |
| erland | | | | | | | | |

| | Danica
Switzerland | Sarah
Switzerland | Islam
Bangladesh | Hanni
Switzerland | Selami
Macedonia | Andrea
Switzerland | Sangeetha
Sri Lanka | Netta
Finland |
| odou
bia | | | | | | | | |

| nes
nany | Rosemarie
Switzerland | Ananthan
Sri Lanka | Pierre
South Africa | Ibrahim
Guinea | Filorete
Serbia | Yoydel
Cuba | | |

Veggie Food – from Weird to Wonderful

The Hiltl story, or why the oldest vegetarian restaurant in Europe is located in Zurich.

First generation

Ambrosius Hiltl (1877–1969) loved everything that was beautiful – opera, nature, good paintings and furniture, fine clothes and travel. He was also remarkably flexible and enterprising, had considerable business talent and a healthy share of self-confidence.

The son of a small farmer in Neumarkt, Bavaria, he was naturally required to learn a trade, in his case that of tailor. After his apprenticeship he set out on his travels as a journeyman because, at that time, artisans were expected to earn their living abroad for a few years. They were supported by their trade associations with a small payment per kilometre travelled. Ambrosius Hiltl's travels took him to Switzerland several times. He earned a living with needle, thread, scissors and thimble in Basel, the Jura area, Geneva, Liestal, Herisau, and Interlaken, before settling in Zurich in the autumn of 1897. He was then 20 years old.

Ambrosius Hiltl

In 1898, the "Vegetarians' Home and Teetotallers' Café" opened in *Stockerstrasse;* because of this unfavourable location it soon moved to *Sihlstrasse*. However, the restaurant was still unsuccessful – on the one hand because of poor management and, on the other, because at that time vegetarians were considered eccentric. It was also difficult to find suitable kitchen staff.

In 1901 Ambrosius Hiltl contracted rheumatoid arthritis. His doctor did not beat about the bush but prophesied an early death if Hiltl did not completely alter his diet and refrain entirely from eating meat.

In those days it was difficult for an unmarried young man to abide by a strict vegetarian diet and still eat tasty and varied food. At the suggestion of a friend, he moved into the *Vegetarierheim* (vegetarians' home). It was a time when the Sunday roast was a status symbol – being able to afford meat showed that one had done well for oneself. Vegetarians were mocked as grass-eaters, and the home was popularly known as *Wurzelbunker*, literally root cellar.

Ambrosius Hiltl was impressed by the vegetarian cuisine and, most important of all, he was cured in a surprisingly short time. For this reason he did not hesitate when the ailing restaurant needed a new manager. It was a tremendous challenge for the tailor from Neumarkt. The daily turnover at the home was then 35 francs, out of which the staff (two kitchen maids, a waitress, and the cook) all had to be paid. The cook, Martha Gneupel, had been raised in a strictly vegetarian family in Saxony; she ran the kitchen and helped serve the guests. Thanks to a steadily growing turnover, Ambrosius Hiltl finally managed to take over the business in 1904. Shortly afterwards he married Martha Gneupel; they had two sons and a daughter.

When Ambrosius Hiltl purchased the property in 1907, his friends asked in amazement: "Why are you buying a house on the outer edge of the city?" There was still a small wood between *Bahnhofstrasse* and *Sihlstrasse* then, and opposite the building was an old cemetery and St. Anna's chapel. In 1909 the Hiltl family became citizens of Zurich and in 1925 the restaurant was refurbished for the first time.

Martha Hiltl-Gneupel

It is interesting to note that, almost at the same time as Hiltl discovered vegetarian cuisine, Dr. Max Bircher-Benner, ten years his senior, opened a clinic to cure his patients with a meat-free diet. Neither Hiltl nor Bircher-Benner fitted the image of dogmatic sectarians. Rather than seeing diet as all important, they saw it in the context of culture and lifestyle. Ambrosius Hiltl was no moralising killjoy. Dr. Ralph Bircher, Max Bircher-Benner's son, in a publication celebrating Hiltl's 90th birthday said: "If you look at Ambrosius Hiltl, the pioneer of vegetarian cuisine, you'll see he is the exact opposite of what people tend to expect of a vegetarian. He is more robust, energetic and jovial than most men at his age, a successful man of the world, and anything but a pale, narrow-chested, unsuccessful and embittered eccentric."

"My grandfather was an open-minded man with many interests. He enjoyed travelling, fraternised with his guests and created an atmosphere in which artists, politicians and

Entrance to the restaurant at the turn of the century

The Hiltl façade from 1931 to 1973

intellectuals in particular felt both relaxed and inspired," This is how Heinz Hiltl remembers his grandfather. This tradition has continued, and the Hiltl restaurant today still hosts celebrities from all walks of life.

Second generation

On her twentieth birthday, in 1926, Margrith Rubli joined the staff of the Hiltl family's vegetarian restaurant as a waitress. On her eightieth birthday she still recalled the conditions of employment applicable at that time. She worked from 7 am to 9.30 pm, with a 1½ hour break during the course of the day. There was half a day off every week and five days holiday a year. She was paid 60 francs a month, plus board and lodging. Even bearing in mind that a cup of coffee only cost 25 cents then, it was not exactly a princely wage.

In 1931 the restaurant was refurbished and the first floor converted into additional dining space. Leonhard Hiltl drew up the plans for the renovation project. He was the older of Ambrosius Hiltl's two sons and later married Margrith Rubli. Leonhard Hiltl had always wanted to be an architect but, in the interests of the family business, he trained as a pastry-cook. It was also in 1931 that he had a fully

The first fully electrified kitchen in Zurich in 1931 – in the Hiltl, of course

electrified industrial kitchen installed in the Hiltl, the first in Zurich. This innovative venture caused a stir well beyond the Swiss catering sector. Leonhard's brother Walter entered the business as chef, and remained at the Hiltl in that capacity for the next 40 years. Most of the recipes still derived from their mother Martha Hiltl. It was a time when vegetarians were regarded with not a little scepticism. They were considered eccentric at the very least. 'A real man eats meat' was the general consensus.

Leonhard Hiltl married Margrith Rubli in 1933, and from then on they jointly ran their vegetarian restaurant with great commitment. In 1951 Margrith Hiltl was the official Swiss delegate to the World Vegetarian Congress in India. Indians regularly frequented the Hiltl because the choice of vegetarian food in conventional Swiss restaurants was minimal, with *rösti* (the Swiss version of hash

The first floor after 1931

browns) or a vegetable platter as the only alternatives to meat. The Hiltl must have seemed like an oasis for them, with Margrith Hiltl always on hand to advise her foreign guests. It is not surprising that friendships gradually developed. And when visiting these friends, Margrith Hiltl gained an insight into the fascinating and diverse Indian cuisine.

She returned full of enthusiasm. What could be better than to put what she had just learnt into practise? She decided that the Hiltl would start to serve Indian dishes forthwith. It was immediately clear to her that this would be a welcome enhancement of the Hiltl menu. However, it was by no means easy to get hold of spices such as curry, coriander, turmeric, cumin and cardamom in the Zurich

of the 1950's, however cosmopolitan the city appeared to be. Indian friends brought these ingredients with them on their visits to

A great honour for Margrith Hiltl: Morarji Desai, the Indian Premier and Finance Minister, dines at the Hiltl.

Switzerland. Moreover, persuading the kitchen staff to prepare Indian dishes was a major stumbling-block. They were convinced that nobody would eat 'such foreign stuff', and refused outright to cook what she requested. This rebuff in no way prevented Margrith Hiltl from carrying out her plans; she prepared the Indian specialities in her private kitchen until one of her cooks took over. Initially, Indian food was only served if ordered in advance. But increasing numbers of Indian guests found their way to the Hiltl, and staff resistance was finally broken when Swissair asked if the Hiltl could supply the food for the airline's Indian passengers.

When Leonhard Hiltl died in 1959 aged 53, Margrith Hiltl took over the management of the restaurant, actively supported by her son Heinz. "The restaurant became a substitute family for her. She was like a mother to her staff", Heinz Hiltl recalls. At the age of eighty Margrith Hiltl was still interested in the business and looked in every day. "But she always let me do what I wanted and did not interfere with the way I ran the business. I shall always be grateful for that."

Third generation

"It certainly wasn't easy for me to play second fiddle, as it were, by letting my son to take over more and more responsibility. After all, when Rolf joined us I was only 53." Heinz Hiltl's reaction to handing over the business to his son is not at all surprising because,

After renovations in 1948

to the very end, his numerous innovations created a stir in the restaurant business.

For once, however, the departure of a senior went very smoothly. "If you have a successor who's charging ahead, then it's wrong to put the brakes on and wait until he's run out of steam."

The years of learning and travel that his son enjoyed after his apprenticeship were just wishful thinking for Heinz Hiltl. His father died when Heinz was only 22, and this meant that he had to help his mother in the business as soon as he had finished his hotel school training course. An interesting parallel is the fact that he, like his son thirty years later, began his Hiltl career by commissioning a survey to find out what kind of people ate vegetarian food on what occasions and why.

The results indicated that, among other things, people under thirty were more likely to change their dietary habits. A young man himself, Heinz Hiltl was convinced that he could attract a younger clientele provided he eliminated the prejudices attached to vegetarian cuisine.

Cover for texts on Ambrosius Hiltl's 90th birthday, by regular guest Alois Carigiet

In 1968 and 1969 Heinz Hiltl attended the first business seminar organised by the Swiss Hotel Association. "It was incredibly exciting. I met many interesting people. The seminar really inspired me and I was simply bursting with new ideas."

In the past few decades the city had expanded so rapidly that the restaurant – once located on the very fringes of the city – was now in the city centre. The guests still came from far and wide, but many also worked in neighbouring office buildings. Reason enough for Heinz Hiltl to make his vision reality.

Hanni and Heinz Hiltl

In 1973, after spectacular renovation and refurbishment, he opened the new Hiltl Vegi. Particularly attractive and a new venture in Zurich's food scene were the salad buffet and the wide selection of fresh natural juices. The 'Indian Tea and Ravaya Corner' on the first floor was a token of respect for his mother, who had silenced all opposition and introduced Indian food into the Hiltl, first for Indian visitors to Zurich, later also for local guests. With its new approach, the Hiltl now catered for a wide market. It differed from other restaurants only in that its menu was exclusively vegetarian and also, perhaps, in that it was a little ahead of its time.

"I deliberately pursued a policy of profit optimisation rather than profit maximisation. I regularly assessed whether my strong commitment to the business was still in line with my personal goals and those of my family, and whether I could take responsibility before God for what I expected from my staff. Success in business was always only one of several goals in my life", is how Heinz Hiltl

sums up his approach. Typically, then, with interests reaching well beyond his own business, Heinz Hiltl was active in various bodies and catering associations. "These other commitments may have been time consuming, but they also served as a source of new ideas and introduced me to many people in the restaurant business."

The restaurant after refurbishment in 1973

The talk of the town: The new façade with its acrylic glass tubes

Fourth generation

Although he was already interested in the family restaurant as a child, Rolf Hiltl (born in 1965) did not want to take the easy road into his father's business. He served his apprenticeship in the kitchens of the Grand Hotel Dolder in Zurich, where the cuisine was in the style of master chef Escoffier – with meat, of course. Rolf was never a strict vegetarian, but despite this he came in for quite a lot of heckling at school because of his parents' business.

After the Dolder he attended the Hotel School in Lausanne, and then spent some time in San Francisco, Acapulco and Paris. Rolf Hiltl had many plans, and he dreamed of opening a restaurant and bar in San Francisco. But it so happened that the Hiltl Restaurant

New Year 1998:
Rolf Hiltl starts into the next millenium

in Zurich – through still popular – had lost some of its élan and could well use a few new ideas and a breath of fresh air. Rolf's father Heinz Hiltl, who had startled his professional peers when he refurbished his business in the early 1970s, did not want to undertake any further innovations without consulting his successor.

His daughter Sonja had become a kindergarten teacher, but his son Rolf abandoned his plans of working abroad. "I think my father sometimes found it difficult to cope with me because I kept changing things and trying something new", he says with a smile. "But then change always takes so long here in Switzerland." Rolf Hiltl's approach is more American than Swiss. He works on the trial and error principle: try something out and then improve on it.

The great-grandson of the founder, Ambrosius Hiltl, could just as well have trusted his instinct: a survey conducted in 1990 confirmed what he knew intuitively. The image of vegetarianism had undergone a fundamental change. A vegetarian was no longer looked upon as someone weird or eccentric who nobly abstained from eating meat, but as someone who enjoyed a different kind of food; in fact, people who eat little or no meat now tend to be trendsetters. Meatless food is no longer sloppy or tasteless food, the very opposite holds true: the modern semi-vegetarian is a connoisseur who combines an enjoyment of food with a healthy diet. And the new approach at the Hiltl provides just that. Good wines and spirits, aromatic teas and coffee are included on the menu as a

matter of course. The refurbished, bistro-style restaurant completed in 1993 clearly reflects Rolf Hiltl's ideas and indicates the new status of vegetarian cuisine.

Opting for a vegetarian restaurant when dining out – almost unthinkable just a few years ago – seems quite natural today. About two-thirds of the people who eat at the Hiltl are women. "Women have always been more health conscious and are always ready to try something new", says Rolf Hiltl. "That's why we focused on increasing the number of male guests via our female clientele." Not without success – more and more men from nearby offices now eat their lunch at the Hiltl.

On 1 January 1998 – one hundred years after the opening of the first vegetarian restaurant in Switzerland – Rolf Hiltl took over the business from his parents and is now solely responsible for running it. At that time he would hardly have believed that vegetarian cuisine would gain popularity so rapidly.

Naturally, a growing number of requests for further Hiltl operations are regularly received from within Switzerland and also from abroad. For various reasons, however, they were always refused. Then in 2000, together with the Frei brothers as partners, the first *tibits by Hiltl* was opened near the Opera in Zurich. There are now already three *tibits* in Switzerland (in Zurich Seefeld, Winterthur and Berne and, from 2007, in Basle). They are all tremendously popular (www.tibits.ch).

In line with the tradition started in 1898, the Hiltl in Zurich's *Sihlstrasse* will continue to be personally run by the Hiltl family. With its growing popularity, Rolf Hiltl had to consider enlarging the restaurant only a few years after the last refurbishment in 1993.

"I find the 2006/2007 construction project fascinating, and am really looking to the opening of our enlarged premises", Rolf Hiltl says. "In future, too, we aim to meld innovation and tradition. There'll be more space, the restaurant will have more generous proportions." The guests will be able to enjoy an

excellent vegetarian meal in a quiet, relaxing atmosphere. Apart from a larger restaurant, the project includes a bar, a banqueting area, a larger takeaway section – and the new Hiltl cookery school.

For its centenary Hiltl had grass growing all over the restaurant's façade

And the next expansion plans? There's nothing definite yet, but Marielle and Rolf Hiltl are raising three small children and, with Céline, Léna and Téo there will be ample opportunities for the fifth generation ...

www.hiltl.ch

The Best Publicity

The Hiltl has served numerous prominent guests. On one page alone of the guest book there are three famous actresses: Käthe Gold, Therese Giehse and Maria Becker. The mayor of Zurich, Emil Klöti, dined here, as did the publicists J.R. von Salis and N.O. Scarpi. The conductors Furtwängler and Stokowsky, the surgeon Sauerbruch, the clown Dimitri, the explorer Auguste Piccard, the dancer Josephine Baker and the film star Hardy Krüger all left their business cards. Margrith Hiltl was particularly impressed by the actor Paul Hubschmid; she told him she always enjoyed watching his films because he kissed so well. Some of the guests also wrote a few friendly (and appreciative) comments. For example Alois Carigiet: «Der Weg zu Hiltl ist für mich eine Einladung an mich selbst: Zu Ruhe und Vernunft.» (For me, going to the Hiltl is an invitation to myself, to an atmosphere of peace and common sense.)

Stephan Eicher, musician

Wenn ich nicht schon fast Vegetarier wäre, würde ich hier einer.
Herzlichen Dank für die asiatische Note im Währschaften, und für das Bodenständige im Orientalischen.
Martin Suter, novelist

«Ich liebe das Hiltl für sein gesundes Essen, die herrlichen Mango-Glacen und das Bio-Bier. Mit dem Herbstteller hatte ich vor Jahren eine ‹love affair› und das Salat-Buffet repräsentiert eine stete Qual der Wahl.»
Hannes B(ühler), fashion designer. We have it on good authority that spelt noodles and red cabbage are among his favourites.

It was great
Gianna Nannini

«Ein exquisites Essen in grosser Auswahl – für Vegetarier eine grosse Seltenheit. Speziell auf Auslandreisen schmerzlich von mir vermisst.»
Nöemi Nadelmann, a well-travelled opera singer from Zurich.

«Ich gehe gern ins Hiltl wegen der frischen, gesunden Küche und vor allem wegen dem feinen und grosszügigen Buffet.»
La Lupa, singer

Es ist uns eine Freude ein hervorragendes Essen in einer wunderbaren Ambiance zu geniessen!! Macht weiter so!!
Natascha Badmann, triathlete

Don't FORGET BAGHDAD
Magnolien blühen,
eine kalte Bise lässt uns frösteln,
ein Diktator fällt,
Donnergrollen weit weg.
Es ist Frühling,
Frühling eines neuen Jahrhunderts.
Hoffen wir auf Demokratie, Gerechtigkeit
und Menschenwürde in der ganzen Welt!
Hiltl-Vegi ist so gesehen eine Bastion
gegen eine globale Mc-Kultur!
Jeder trägt dazu bei, Sorgfalt im
Umgang mit der Welt aufzubauen.
Mit Speisen und mit Filmen…
Samir, film director

«Als ein guter Freund, ein Inder-Tamil, sagte, er
gehe nach Genf an ein Familienfest und freue sich
auf das Buffet, spöttelte ich: Wie reich kann schon
ein vegetarisches Buffet sein. Zur Belehrung lud
er mich ins Hiltl ein. Was alles auf den Teller
kommen konnte, brachte mich von meiner
falschen Meinung ab. Seither geht es mir wie
meinem Bekannten, ich freue mich auf das Buffet, nicht mehr aus pädagogischen Gründen, sondern aus kulinarischen.»
Hugo Loetscher, novelist

«Einfach jederzeit super im Hiltl – man geht voll
Energie von hier weg.»
Vera Kaa, singer

When it comes to this restaurant, I am not neutral. I have a clear position: excellent.
Avraham Hirschson, Israeli MP

Pesto heaven!
Jimmi Sommerville, musician

If it grows, you feed it to people in the most
wonderful way: in a healthy and pleasant way.
See you next time.
*Israel Singer, from the World Jewish Congress. His
Swiss wife visited the Hiltl with her parents when
she was a child, and she loved it even then.*

Sina, singer

Just returned from a European trip, ate in
marvellous 3 & 4 star restaurants, London, Paris,
Burgundy, Alsace, Provence, Munich, Rome, and
on the Crystal Harmony Ship – and the best food
we had was at Hiltl.
Understand, I love meat. I was raised by German
parents in the USA and we had meat 3 times a
day. But your restaurant is so innovative and well
run and the food is so delicious I could easily become a vegetarian if I lived in Zurich. And the
waitresses are so pleasant and happy it must
reflect your good management.
Are you interested in opening a Hiltl in Beverly
Hills? Or Brentwood? It would be inundated
with customers, you would have lines of people
waiting to get in.
*David Swift, film producer, director and script-
writer in L.A. (Films starring Jack Lemmon, Jodie
Foster, Glenn Ford, David Niven, Romy Schneider).*

Thank you very much for a wonderful evening. Hope to see you in London soon.
Anton Mosimann

Vom höchsten Punkt im Kanton Zürich habe ich das «Hiltl» auch ohne Kompass gefunden... Es war hervorragend!
Simone Luder-Niggli, orienteering world champion

Besten Dank für die Einladung im Namen der ganzen «Compania». Ich wünsche Ihnen alles Gute im kommenden Jahr.
Jimmi Sommerville, musician

Thanks for a fabulous "veggie" meal.

Great service, food, and ambience.

LONG MAY YOU PROSPER!......
Paul McCartney
.... and expand !!

Heather McCartney

3. 06. 04.

Paul McCartney, Heather McCartney

Wieso hat Hiltl noch nicht die fleischlose Apfelröschti im Angebot?
... man kann ja nicht alles – aber Hiltl kann viel!
Emil

«Die vegetarische Küche des Hiltl ist in ihrer Vielfalt kaum zu übertreffen. Zu hoffen ist trotzdem, dass der Erfolg nicht noch grösser wird, weil sonst selbst um zehn Uhr nachts kaum noch ein freier Tisch zu finden ist.»
Paul Reichsteiner, Swiss MP

«Salud pasta y buena lechuga. Nos vemos otra vez.»
Heroes del Silencio, rock band

Well what can i say one of the finest vegetable selection ever. The food, the place, ambiance, atmosphere, talks.
We'll love to come again and again and again. Very friendly, smiling and pleasure staff.
Mayur Verma, Bollywood star

«Besonderes Essen in unkompliziert-lockerer Atmosphäre führt uns immer wieder mal ins Hiltl: Begeistert bin ich vom vielfältigen, kreativen Salatbuffet, das in Zürich einmalig ist. Ich schätze aber auch die Suppen, die Rösti und die Pâtisserie – alles tagesfrisch. Vegetarisch essen ist im Hiltl keine Religion, sondern ein Genuss. So vielfältig wie die Gerichte sind auch die Gäste. Eine buntgemischte Schar, viele junge Leute und flinkes, freundliches Personal sorgen jeden Tag für frische Laune.»
As befits his former office, Josef Estermann, mayor of Zurich, has the last word.

Hiltl Catering

Hiltl's vegetarian specialities and titbits are always popular at larger events in Zurich and elsewhere. We provide an appetizing alternative to the range of grilled meats generally available at major festivals, rock concerts, open-air cinemas and similar. Whether it's a public celebration or private party, we'll cater for it – indoors or out.

Hiltl

189

On the Advantages of a Vegetarian Diet

Scientific proof that their diet makes vegetarians healthier has been available for about ten years. Carefully controlled studies of vegetarians have shown that a diet without meat and fish but, instead, with plenty of vegetables, fruit, and cereal products as well as with milk and eggs not only ensures that there are no deficiencies but, in fact, has significant advantages.

Almost all the risk factors for such common diet-dependent diseases as high blood pressure, heart attacks, diabetes mellitus, gout, and similar are notably less prominent among vegetarians than among people who favour a mixed diet. On average, vegetarians are two-thirds less likely to get cancer. It has lately also been shown that vegetarians live longer. The basic reason for all this is that vegetarian food tends to be low in calories – there are hardly any overweight vegetarians – and it is also lower in fat and cholesterol. As a result, the likelihood of vegetarians suffering a heart attack is 60 percent lower. At the same time, a vegetarian diet contains almost all the essential nutrients in the quantity recommended (in vain) by national and international dietary councils. The high fibre intake of about 40 g per day not only ensures active, normal digestion, but also helps to prevent many diseases of modern society. The inclusion of milk provides a stable supply of biologically valuable protein as well as sufficient vitamin B12.

Professor Helmut Rottka,
Dr. med.
Freie Universität Berlin

An Award-winning Concept

Hiltl even collects awards for its advertising;
its food and hospitality are already legendary, anyway.

The New York Festivals, International Print Advertising, 1994

Swiss Corporate Design award, 1994/95

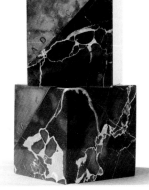

Silver from the Art Directors Club 2002/2003

Marcellino's Restaurant Report 1998 / guest award

left:
Guinness Book of Records, 1998

centre:
Mérite Brasserie + Bistro 1997

right:
Finalist award winner, advertising spot "Hunt", 2005

Edi 2003, Swiss advertising film prize, best concept

Gold laurels 2002, Hiltl cookery book

Hiltl – the number 1 abroad, too

Hiltl

191

Hiltl's Original Advertising

Seit 99 Jahren
kein Fleisch.
Nicht einmal
eine Fliege in
der Suppe.

Wohl das beste vegetarische Restaurant mitten in Zürich.

Hiltl

Since 100 years:
a bloody good
restaurant.

Das älteste vegetarische Restaurant in Zürich feiert seinen 100. Geburtstag.

Hiltl
Seit 1898

Jetzt gibts erstmals
Open Airs, an denen
mehr Pflänzchen
gegessen als
geraucht werden.

Hiltl

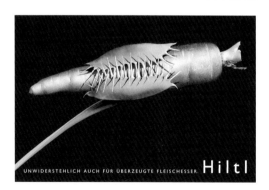

UNWIDERSTEHLICH AUCH FÜR ÜBERZEUGTE FLEISCHESSER. **Hiltl**

Hiltl
VEGETARIAN RESTAURANT.

Leidenschaftlicher
Vegetarier?

A vegetarian diet clears the head and stimulates the brain.
To remove any remaining doubts we recommend a stroll through
our website: www.hiltl.ch, and a relaxed look at our advertising.